NEW ZEALAND
TREASURE WRECKS

For my daughters

Zephanie, Nicola and Kerry

NEW ZEALAND TREASURE WRECKS

Steve Locker-Lampson

The
Halcyon
Press

ACKNOWLEDGMENTS

Most of the treasure recovered from the shipwrecks mentioned in this book, and many of the other artifacts, were salvaged between 1966 and 1985 by teams led by the late Kelly Tarlton for his Museum of Shipwrecks aboard the converted sugar lighter, *Tui*, situated at Waitangi in the Bay of Islands. All of these items are now on display in the museum.

Without the co-operation of museum owner, Rosemary Tarlton, and manager, Frank Kowalewski, it would have been quite impossible for me to produce this book. Information, access to Kelly's photographic files and permission to photograph the relevant displays was invaluable. To Rosemary and Frank, my heartfelt thanks for your help and your trust.

There were many others who also contributed to this book and I would like to express my gratitude to them as well, particularly to Ian Francis who collaborated with me on earlier books and continues to inspire me; Malcolm Blair for his continuing readiness to supply me with information and photographs; John Dearling for information and photographs; Quentin Bennett and Chris Glasson, whose superb underwater photographs and unstinting support have always been freely given; Jessica Cowley for her hand-drawn maps; Dr Kim Morgan for her endless encouragement and practical help and to all the others who have contributed to a greater or lesser extent.

Thank you all.

Published by

The Halcyon Press.

A division of

Halcyon Publishing Ltd.

C.P.O. Box 360, Auckland New Zealand.

Printed by

Colorcraft Ltd,
Hong Kong

Typeset by

Typeset Graphics ISBN 0-908685-23-8

Contents

INTRODUCTION

What constitutes treasure? Chambers' Twentieth Century Dictionary states that it is "anything much valued" and, as such, almost every vessel that has been sunk since man first set forth in a hollowed-out log could be regarded as a treasure wreck - even hollowed-out logs were valuable when the work had to be done with primitive hand tools. Nowadays, of course, the older the vessel the more value it has to archaeologists and historians, and about the only 'wrecks' that have no value at all are the more recent hulks that had finished their useful lives, been partially dismantled and deliberately sunk to get rid of them. On most of these nothing is left but rusting iron and rotting timber.

However, for the purpose of this book I am considering 'Treasure Wrecks' to mean those vessels that sank while carrying cargoes, personal possessions or stores of some intrinsic value – though time may well have increased that value a hundredfold – and am ignoring the fact that some of the vessels themselves could be of historical interest.

We do not have, sunk round New Zealand's coastline, any Spanish galleons loaded with glittering cargoes of precious metals and jewels as were wrecked in the waters of the British Isles and the Caribbean. Some of these have been re-located and many millions of dollars worth of treasure taken from them. Nor do we have the silver-carrying Dutch East Indiamen as have been discovered and excavated off the coast of Western Australia.

Our short history and geographical location have ensured that our treasure wrecks are not on quite the same scale but, none-the-less, some carried extremely valuable cargoes either because of rarity or because of their intrinsic worth.

Treasure hunting on wrecks is fraught with difficulties, not the least of which are the legal rights to anything found. The laws relating to treasure salvage are extremely complex and should be looked into thoroughly before commencing any sort of salvage work. Very briefly, ANYTHING recovered must be reported to the Receiver of Wreck.

Many people in Europe, the West Indies and America have excavated shipwrecks and recovered hundreds of thousands, even millions, of dollar's worth of treasure only to find that the State has the rights to what they have found and can dictate exactly what is to be done with the recovered artifacts, regardless of whether the salvor gains by it or not; and when a salvage operator has spent all his money on the search and recovery he is not likely to find it very amusing.

Tom Gurr, one of the better known Florida treasure hunters, after salvaging gold, silver, jewellery and other artifacts from the wreck of a Spanish galleon, discovered that the State wanted to totally control it – so he took the whole lot back out to sea and dumped it overboard under the watchful eyes of a television news crew that he had hired for the occasion. He was then taken to court by the

State for Grand Larceny – you cannot always win!

Kip Wagner spent years researching, searching for and eventually excavating the wrecks of the 1715 Spanish plate fleet and was later joined by Mel Fisher who went on to recover the riches of the *Nuestra Senora de Atocha*. Every cent Fisher owned or could borrow went into the hunt and it's said at one time he was so broke he had to pay for his groceries with Spanish 'pieces of eight'. When he found gold it was all tied up so tightly in legal wrangles that he could not recoup any of his losses for a long time. Again it was the Florida State authorities that made life difficult for him and it was not until he finally found the bulk of the treasure that he made any profit at all. The legal arguments went on for years but eventually the international laws relating to treasure salvage were changed more in keeping with the realities of modern salvage costs and Mel Fisher is now a wealthy man. It is believed that over $40,000,000 worth of treasure came out of the *Atocha* alone – but was it worth it? One of his sons and his daughter-in-law died when the salvage tug capsized mysteriously while close to the wreck site.

A more recent treasure wreck was that of HMS *Edinburgh* which left Murmansk on convoy duty on 29 April, 1942, with four and a half tons of gold in her bomb room. This bullion was payment from the Russians to the British and Americans for war supplies.

On 30 April the *Edinburgh* was torpedoed twice and left helpless before enemy warships also attacked her. Dead in the water she was deliberately sunk by the Royal Navy to stop the enemy getting their hands on the gold.

After several planned, but never executed, expeditions to salvage the *Edinburgh's* bullion salvage company, Jessop Marine, secured the contract in 1981 and within ten days of starting the search for the wreck, found her in 245 metres of water off the north coast of Norway.

On 15 September, 1981 the first gold bar was recovered and by 7 October – only three weeks later – the company had salvaged 431 of the 465 bars that had been shipped on the vessel. This was a staggering feat considering the depth and coldness of the water and must rate as one of the most successful salvages ever attempted. In total the recovered gold was worth, in 1981, £43,000,000 of which the salvage company received 45%, the remaining 55% going to the British and Russian governments.

Until relatively recently treasure seekers were almost always after precious metals or jewellery. This changed dramatically in 1985 when a team led by Captain Mike Hatcher located the 1751 wreck of the *Geldermansen*, a Dutch East Indiaman, east of Singapore and recovered from her remains more than 180,000 pieces of blue and white porcelain that had been under forty metres of water for 234 years. Although destined for the middle-class dinner tables of Europe this porcelain was not considered of great commercial value at the time of shipping and was used almost as ballast for the light cargo of tea that was the vessel's more important cargo. It was packed in these cases of tea for protection and was still in near perfect condition in 1985. When sold by public auction in Amsterdam in 1986 it fetched far more than the salvors had believed possible; over £10,000,000 sterling!

Mike Hatcher was also involved in a less rewarding incident in the Gulf of Thailand. He had located and was excavating a 12th century vessel loaded with pottery urns, dishes and figurines from ancient Siam when the Thai police and navy stepped in and forced him, under pain of arrest and probable imprisonment, to hand over millions of dollars worth of artifacts that he had recovered.

This was basically an act of piracy on the part of the Thai authorities as the wreck was lying in international waters but, under the guns of the naval craft, he had no option but to comply with their demands.

Another problem with treasure wrecks is that as soon as they have been located the 'vultures' move in and some very ugly situations have arisen. Underwater sites are virtually impossible to police full time, for obvious reasons, and as soon as the legal salvage crew leaves the site anyone can dive in the area. The sea is free and who is to say that someone has picked up a few coins from the bottom? Some coins from these wrecks are worth more than $20,000 each on the open market!

All the successful treasure hunters are dedicated fanatics and have to be to achieve their success. It is a long hard road to the glittering prizes that wait for man underwater and the hunt can demand great sacrifices. It is frequently dangerous work and always expensive; few people ever make it but for those who do the rewards can be beyond even their wildest dreams.

In 1976 I was taken to a wreck site that had produced gold coins and, although not expecting to find anything of any value, started to fan away the shingle on the sea floor. Within five minutes I found a one-hundred-and-ten-year-old gold sovereign and the thrill of finding that first gold coin is indescribable. Gold is quite unmistakable and when I first saw it among the swirling debris that I had stirred up I knew instantly what it was. That one sovereign is now worth approximately NZ$1,500, more than 500 times its face value of £1 stirling! That is treasure!

Steve Locker-Lampson – 1995

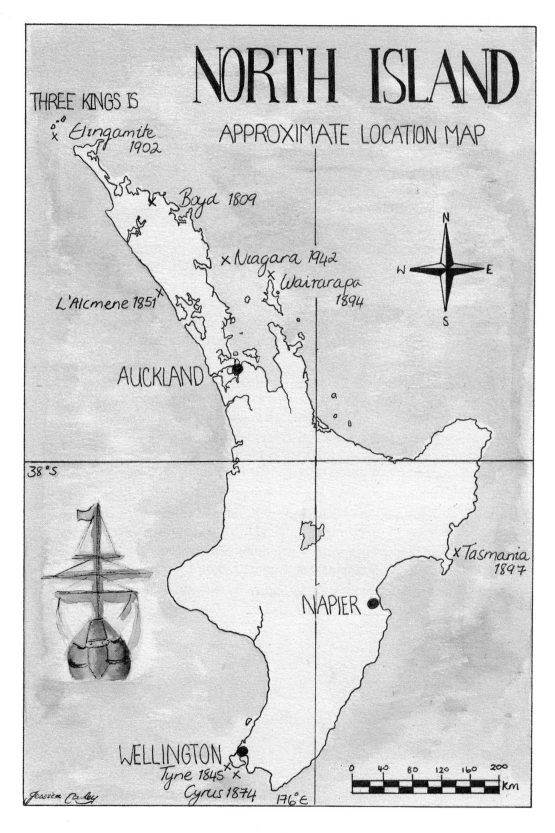

NORTH ISLAND
APPROXIMATE LOCATION MAP

THREE KINGS IS

x Elingamite 1902

Boyd 1809

x Niagara 1942

x Wairarapa 1894

L'Alcmene 1851 x

AUCKLAND

N
W · E
S

38°S

x Tasmania 1897

NAPIER

WELLINGTON
Tyne 1845 x
Cyrus 1874
176°E

Jessica Bailey

0 40 80 120 160 200
km

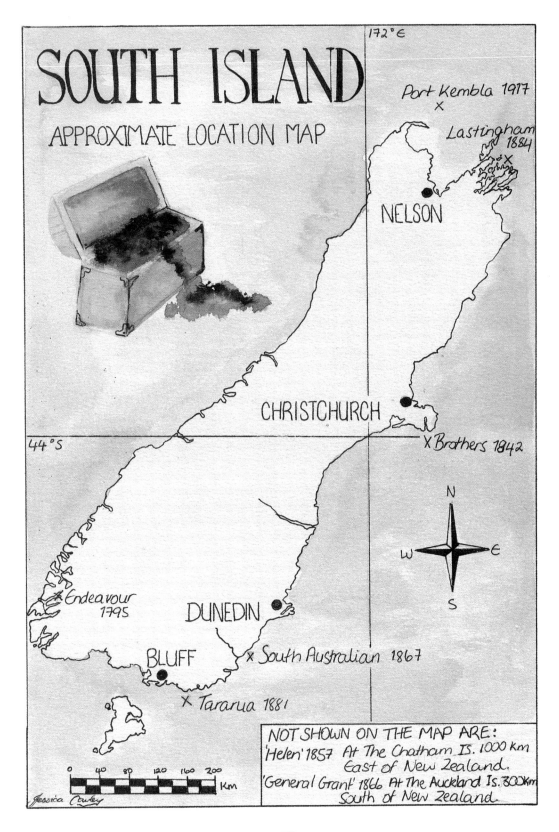

SOUTH ISLAND

APPROXIMATE LOCATION MAP

172°E

Port Kembla 1917
X

Lastingham 1884
X

NELSON

CHRISTCHURCH

44°S

X Brothers 1842

N
W   E
S

Endeavour 1795

DUNEDIN

BLUFF

X South Australian 1867

X Tararua 1881

NOT SHOWN ON THE MAP ARE:
'Helen' 1857 At The Chatham Is. 1000 km East of New Zealand.
'General Grant' 1866 At The Auckland Is. 300 km South of New Zealand.

0   40   80   120   160   200
Km

Jessica Cowley

13

CHAPTER ONE

THE MINOR TREASURE WRECKS

The ship *Boyd* burning in Whangaroa harbour, Northland, in 1809. From a painting by Walter Wright. (Alexander Turnbull Library).

A good example of treasure with rarity value in New Zealand is, in the mid-1970s, when several sovereigns were found off Owhiro Bay, Wellington, in four metres of water where the barque *Cyrus* and full-rigged ship *Wellington* were wrecked on 7 March, 1874. The actual wreck that produced these sovereigns is not known for certain as both, being wooden ships on an exposed coast, have virtually ceased to exist; but it is believed that it is the *Cyrus*. The number of coins found is also in dispute, seventeen sovereigns and one half-sovereign were declared to the authorities but newspaper reports in 1976 stated that over forty had been found.

All these coins are in exceptionally good condition and in 1995 were worth between $500 and $5,000 each to collectors, the Sydney mint ones being of the greatest value. If, as I believe, at least thirty five coins were recovered and the average value is only $1,000 they would now be worth $35,000; not a great fortune but well worth the trouble of the search – and this vessel was not known to have been carrying specie.

But treasure does not have to be gold, silver or precious stones – although this is usually the case – and the earliest recorded New Zealand shipwreck, the *Endeavour*, taken to Facile Harbour, Dusky Sound in an unseaworthy state during October 1795, was reputed to have greenstone (nephrite jade) for ballast. Over eighty years after the accident, in 1878, Captain Fairchild of the Government steamer *Hinemoa* visited the wreck site and stated in his report, "The ship had greenstone and chalk for ballast . . .", but the earlier journal of Robert Murray, the third officer of the *Endeavour* on her last voyage, states for Monday 14 October, 1795: "The day was well occupied in heaving the ballast out", and on the next day, "We were employed as before". The *Endeavour* had, at this stage, been moored in Facile Harbour to find out how extensive the leaks were and presumably a considerable portion of the ballast would have had to be removed for this purpose. At 2am on 27 October, 1795 the vessel somehow "struck against a rock" whilst still moored and was beached in a sinking condition. On the same day Murray wrote, "The morning was occupied in shifting our berth and the afternoon getting ballast out." If Captain Fairchild knew what he was talking about and the ballast really was greenstone, then there must be a pile of it on the bottom of Facile Harbour as well as some possibly still in the mouldering remains of the vessel that lie where she was beached two hundred years ago. Captain Fairchild also believed that the *Endeavour* was Captain Cook's ship of the same name so he could easily have been wrong in the matter of the greenstone as well!

The greenstone rumour has persisted, however, despite many fruitless expeditions to the site in recent years. Who really knows what lies beneath the cold waters of Dusky Sound? Maybe in the future someone will make their fortune from the discarded ballast; greenstone is worth a great deal of money these days and would certainly be considered treasure.

Before the *Endeavour* was beached the crew unloaded many of the ship's stores by the use of rafts and boats and two iron cannon were accidentally lost overboard in the transfer. Both of these were recovered in 1984 by a team led by Dr Simon Cotton and Kelly Tarlton.

Another early treasure wreck was that of the *Boyd*. In December 1809 she was burned to the water-line (and all but four of the passengers and crew are believed to have been killed and eaten by the Maori) while lying at anchor in Whangaroa Harbour to load kauri spars.

A persistent rumour has followed her down through the years that when the Maori sacked her they carried off in one of their canoes a chest full of money. According to Eugene Grayland in his *Coasts of Treachery* this money, £30,000, was the property of one of the passengers who was killed but, though it is likely,

On an 1836 chart the wreck of the *Boyd* is shown south of Red Island. (Auckland Institute & Museum).

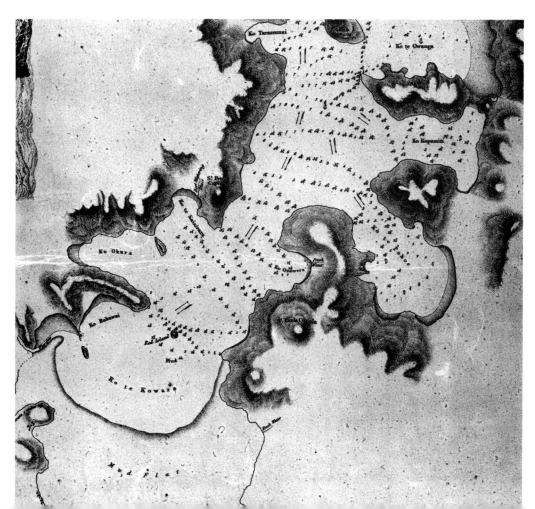

it has never been substantiated that he had this money with him when he sailed in the *Boyd.*

The canoe carrying the plunder, however, is reported to have capsized depositing the treasure chest in the mud of the mangrove swamps at the upper end of the harbour, from which it has never been recovered.

The rumour as to its loss appears to have come from the Maori themselves but seems to be rather vague, and the only other evidence was that some Maori were later seen wearing *Boyd* coins hung round their necks – but these could have come from anywhere in the vessel and not necessarily from the treasure chest.

Well-known Paihia treasure diver, the late Kelly Tarlton, researched this wreck thoroughly and said that, if there ever was money on the vessel it was probably not in coin form but more likely to have been bank drafts of some sort. I am not totally convinced of this even though £30,000 in gold would have taken up considerable space, and believe that if this money was on board it could well have been gold – paper money of any sort was still vaguely distrusted at that time and a man liked to have something more substantial to show for his labours. Where it is however, is anybody's guess and it will probably never be found considering the nature of the harbour and its surrounds, although, a man told me in 1981 that he knew the area where this treasure was and had every intention of finding it with the aid of a metal detector.

Some other vague rumours also give accounts of the money having been carried ashore and buried at a variety of places; the slopes of Mt. Taratara, behind the Whangaroa Hotel and on Mt. Kaeo. As with all rumours (and the mention of treasure seems to breed them) there is usually at least a grain of truth in them and if the £30,000 was in gold it could now be worth several million dollars!

Another wreck that has delivered up a 'much valued' artifact is that of the French corvette *L'Alcmene*, wrecked on Bayleys Beach between Hokianga and Kaipara in 1851. She was not carrying bullion or any other valuable cargo but did have on board something much sought-after by Kelly Tarlton – bronze swivel guns. Tarlton had no idea that these were on board when he and Noel Hilliam started a routine search of the wreck in 1977, and was just searching for artifacts for his museum.

Their initial dive turned up a corroded mass of iron and, close by, the top of an anchor; adhering to the mass was the first swivel gun. Tarlton told reporters afterwards, "I have long dreamed of finding a bronze cannon, but never thought for one minute I would discover one here." They later found a second swivel gun and recovered several other artifacts including a one tonne iron cannon. Maybe this should not be considered as treasure in the strictest sense of the word but to Tarlton it was an extremely valuable find.

Another intriguing rumour is that the *Lastingham*, wrecked near Cape Jackson in 1884, had four hundred sovereigns in her safe. I find this intriguing because I can find no trace of where the rumour originated, it seems to have suddenly come to light in the 1960s when the wreck was first visited by divers. However, from all available evidence, the safe has never been located and it might well contain gold. The four hundred sovereigns would be worth a minimum of $200 each and probably considerably more. The remains of the *Lastingham* were discovered in 1967 and since then it and the nearby *Rangitoto* have become a mecca for divers and are frequently visited. Few people come away from the *Lastingham* empty-handed, even if it is only with an old bottle, and the wreck has been thoroughly searched many times but, for some reason, nobody has yet come across the safe. Is it still there? Has someone surreptitiously removed it, or did it never really exist? Even if it did exist and is still among the crumbling remains there is no guarantee that it holds anything of any value and the finder could be very disappointed.

The barque *Tyne* sank by the Rimurapa Rocks near Wellington on 4 July, 1845 with, among other things, six cases of gold on board, the loss of which was said at the time to have been a "Colonial calamity".

During the ensuing weeks five of these cases were recovered from the wreck by the use of an ingenious device, basically a tapering screw on the end of a long shaft. When a case of bullion had been located this tool would be screwed into the top and the case hauled to the surface.

Of the sixth case there is some doubt as to whether it was ever found as there do not appear to be any reports concerning it, which is unusual in itself as recovery of the first five was covered in some detail in the local newspapers and the missing four hundred pounds was a great deal of money in those days. As with all treasure rumours abound concerning this sixth case, the strongest of which implies that it may well have been the foundation of the fortunes of a prominent early settler in the area. On the other hand it may well still be underwater somewhere near Rimurapa Rocks. After the vessel was wrecked she broke in two and the separate halves drifted in opposite directions along the coast; on which part the gold was is not mentioned which makes the search even more difficult. The bow section was eventually washed ashore and it and its contents sold by public auction on the beach but whether the stern section drifted east or west is uncertain.

A diver reported seeing what he thought was part of a mast in the vicinity in the mid-1970s and, although it is unlikely, this could possibly have been from the *Tyne*, but two of her masts were cut away before she was wrecked so this information could be misleading. Apart from that the wreckage, to my knowledge, has not been found although some divers have mentioned seeing small pieces of copper sheathing and other artifacts in widely different places on the same part of the coast.

Now it would be an extremely difficult task to pinpoint the wreck site – wooden ships do not last long on the extremely exposed southern coast and the only indications would probably be a few bronze fittings, small pieces of copper sheathing and, possibly, the unmistakeable gleam of gold!

Another lesser-known wreck that I consider still to be a treasure wreck is that of the *Helen*. There is little available written evidence that the treasure on this vessel was ever recovered but that does not mean that it is still there for the taking. The wreck has been known about for a long time and it seems inconceivable to me that no one has ever tried to recover the gold that was known to have been on board, either shortly after the accident or in more recent times.

The *Helen* was a wooden brigantine that was swept onto a lee shore while anchored off Waieri in the Chatham Islands in July 1857, due to what was described at the time as a hurricane. Three men who were aloft at the time were the only ones saved, the remainder of the crew being drowned. The survivors were thrown by the force of the sea onto a ledge in the cliffs.

Such was the severity of the storm that the following morning there was nothing visible left of the brigantine except for flotsam and the dead bodies of her crew.

The interesting part of her story, as far as treasure is concerned, is that in C.W.N. Ingram's *New Zealand Shipwrecks* it is mentioned that, apart from the cargo of 150 bushels of oats and a few casks of oil, there was cash on board to the value of about £650. If this cash was in the form of gold, as would be almost certain, and if it has not since been recovered, then the value today would be almost a quarter of a million dollars! However, there is a steep drop-off at the entrance to the small bay where she was wrecked and if the remains have been washed over this she could be in very deep water.

On 10 November, 1842 the 44 ton cutter *Brothers* was capsized by a squall while off Manukatahi inside Akaroa heads, with three hundred sovereigns on board. The master, Captain James Bruce is said to have been rescued by a Maori woman, whom he then kept in food and clothes for the rest of her life. However, all accounts of this wrecking are rather confused and seem to be mixed between two vessels, the other being the 1844 loss of the *Magnet*, also wrecked at Akaroa, while under the command of Captain Lewis. The on-board money has also been attributed to both vessels although it is believed that it was on the *Brothers*. No records refer to any recovery of the missing gold.

On 2 April, 1867 the steamer *South Australian* ran aground at Coal Point, north of the Clutha River, on the east coast of the South Island. In *The Atlas Of Shipwrecks and Treasure* written by Englishman Nigel Pickford and published in 1994 (supposed to be the 'definitive' book on the subject) it is stated that the *South Australian* had on board, "Cargo: Gold. Largely salvaged at time of loss". The 'largely' is interesting because it means that some could still remain – but how much and where the wreck lies are, at this time, anybody's guess.

However, the aforementiond book also mentions several other New Zealand treasure wrecks and much of the information appears incorrect. The *Tararua* (spelt *Taranua*) is said to have been carrying gold as a cargo which it was not (see Chapter 6). The *Tyne* had six cases of gold on board as opposed to the stated five cases, and the *Tasmania* (see chapter 8) is not mentioned at all. Also, for this 'definitive' 1994 book, as far as New Zealand is concerned the information seems to stop in the 1960s as no mention is made of the many later recoveries of treasure or the fruitless expeditions set up for this purpose.

The *Rangitane* was a large motor vessel carrying 111 passengers and about 200 crew when she left Auckland on 24 November, 1940. Included in her cargo was a consignment of silver.

On the morning of 27 November the *Rangitane* was approached by no less than three German raiders, the *Orion, Komet* and *Kulmerland,* but the New Zealand Steamship Company's vessel managed to radio her plight to the authorities before the enemy opened fire. The attack has been described in British accounts as "savage and ruthless" and continued even after the vessel had stopped, killing at least ten of those on board and wounding many others. The book written by the commander of the *Orion,* Kurt Weyher, and Hans Jurgen Ehrlich in 1955 and entitled *The Black Raider,* however, paints a different picture and indicates that no ship fired on the *Rangitane* after she had stopped transmitting and that only eight people were killed, four passengers and four crew, three of whom died later from their wounds. (In World War I the practice had been for raiders to signal their victims not to use their radios and, because few of these merchant vessels carried either radios or guns they usually surrendered without a fight. In World War II most ships were equipped with both and it was therefore necessary to eliminate the threat as soon as possible. As Kurt Weyher said: "A scrupulous observation of the unwritten laws of the chivalrous code of sailors would in many cases have been equivalent to suicide; in the age of radio the hunter so easily becomes the hunted.)

After survivors had been taken aboard the enemy ships the *Rangitane* was attacked by torpedoes and shells and sank in position 36°48'S latitude, 175°27'W longitude, some 300 nautical miles east of East Cape.

Whether the Germans removed the forty five bars of silver bullion from the vessel before sinking her is unknown and not recorded in *THE BLACK RAIDER.* The wreck is however in very deep water, some 7,800 metres! But who knows whether future technology will one day place this treasure within the reach of man.

A few other vessels have also been lost, outward bound from New Zealand, including the full rigged ship *Matoaka* which sailed from Lyttelton on 13 May, 1869 and disappeared with 77 people on board. On her cargo manifest was gold. And the *Glenmark,* another full rigged ship, that left New Zealand in early 1872 with fifty passengers and crew and £80,000 worth of gold stowed in her strongroom. Both of these vessels were only reported as "missing" so no one knows where they are, but there is always the possibility that they were wrecked soon after leaving the coast and not inconceivable that someone will eventually stumble across their remains.

On 16 February 1986 the Russian liner *Mikhail Lermontov* struck rocks at Cape Jackson in the Marlborough Sounds and sank soon afterwards in Port Gore.

At the time of the accident – which has never been satisfactorily explained – the vessel was carrying a full complement of passengers and crew all but one of whom made it to safety. The body of the missing crew member has never been found.

Some time after the vessel went down Divers World Salvage Ltd were contracted to recover the ship's safes and the gold contents of the duty free shop on board. By the time thay had finished they had recovered over $70,000 worth of money and valuables. Left on board the wreck there must be a considerable quantity of personal effects that could be worth many thousands of dollars, particularly in the baggage hold. However, this is a dangerous wreck to enter and three divers have already lost their lives while exploring her massive hull.

Other wrecks on the New Zealand coast have yielded gold to the dedicated wreck diver; rings, collar studs, watch chains, tie pins, lockets and coins have all

Two rings recovered from a passenger cabin on the Russian liner, *Mikhail Lermontov*. These together with other jewellery were returned to their owner by the salvors. (Malcolm Blair).

been found but not usually in sufficient quantity to be classed as treasure. They make interesting and valuable souvenirs and are rarely reported to the authorities as the law demands, mainly because the finders are afraid that the objects will be taken off them with no compensation. In fact, this is not the case and to use the *Cyrus* again as an example, one man who found some of the sovereigns declared his find and of fifteen coins the Government took four for museums and paid him the current market value for them, the remaining eleven coins were returned to him.

It usually pays to observe the law in these matters as they are difficult secrets to keep and if there is any suspicion that someone has undeclared goods recovered from a wreck the Receiver of Wreck has considerable powers and can search homes without a warrant if he has cause to believe that the owner is harbouring undisclosed artifacts.

Another law that pertains to the removal of anything from shipwrecks, and should be carefully noted, is the Historic Places Act 1993 of which the following are the relevant excerpts.

2. "Archaeological site" means any place in New Zealand that –

(ii) Is the site of the wreck of any vessel where that wreck occurred before 1900.

10. Archaeological sites not to be destroyed, damaged, or modified –

(1) Except pursuant to an authority granted under section 14 of this Act, it shall not be lawful for any person to destroy, damage, or modify, or cause to be destroyed, damaged, or modified, the whole or any part of any archaeological site, knowing or having reasonable cause to suspect that it is an archaeological site.

(2) Except as provided in section 15 or in section 18 of this Act, it shall not be lawful for any person to carry out any archaeological investigation that may destroy, damage, or modify any archaeological site.

11. Application to destroy, damage, or modify archaeological site –

(1) Any person wanting to destroy, damage, or modify the whole or any part of any archaeological site shall first apply to the Trust for an authority to do so.

97. Offence of intentional destruction, damage, or modification –

(1) Every person commits an offence who intentionally –

(a) Destroys, damages, or modifies any historic place, historic area, property, or thing vested in or under the control of the Trust; or

(b) Causes any such area, place, property, thing, or land to be destroyed, damaged, or modified, –

without the authority of the Trust or any person or body authorised by the Trust in that behalf.

(2) Every person who commits an offence against subsection

(1) of this section is liable on summary conviction, –

(a) In the case of destruction, to a fine not exceeding $100,000:

(b) In the case of damage or modification, to a fine not exceeding $40,000.

Seventeen sovereigns, one ½ sovereign and two silver coins from the wreck of what is believed to have been the *Cyrus*. (S.L-L)

A few of the silver coins found on the remains of the *Tararua*. (Chris Glasson).

Two of the *Tararua* coins. (Chris Glasson).

Wade Doak reaches for a pile of silver coins 44m down on the *Elingamite*. Two gold half sovereigns are in his mask for safe keeping. (Kelly Tarlton).

Sorting partially cleaned *Elingamite* coins. (Kelly Tarlton).

CHAPTER TWO

PORT KEMBLA

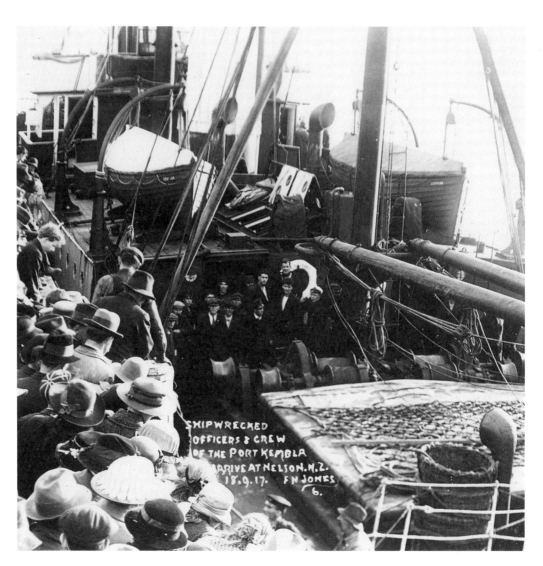

Survivors of the World War I victim, ss *Port Kembla,* aboard the *Regulus* on arrival at Nelson. (Jones collection − Alexander Turnbull Library).

The *Port Kembla* is another wreck that is not associated with the general conception of what treasure should be. She carried no gold or silver or jewellery to her watery grave off Cape Farewell and yet, in her rotting hull, there lies a fortune for someone who has the technical expertise and the funds to set up a salvage operation.

In the early morning of September 18, 1917, the *Port Kembla* was rocked by an explosion that ripped a hole in the starboard side of the forward hold causing her to rapidly fill with water. Within half an hour the vessel had sunk leaving two lifeboats bobbing in the water where she had been.

The lifeboats, containing all fifty nine members of the crew, were sighted some five hours later by the steamer *Regulus* and taken in tow for Nelson where they were landed about midday on September 18 – eleven hours after the explosion – to the excitement of a large crowd that had gathered on the wharf. Because of wartime restrictions it was not immediately made known which vessel it was that had sunk although it is hard to imagine that the Nelson crowd would not have found out very quickly from members of the crew.

Some time after the sinking of the *Port Kembla* the master, Captain J. Jack, stated that he was convinced that the explosion had been internal and must have been the work of saboteurs. During World War I he was not alone in this assumption and the later enquiry into the loss came to the conclusion that, in the opinion of the court, this was the case and was due to the placing of a quantity of high explosives in the hold. No culprit was ever brought to light however, and when an enemy minefield was subsequently found in the vicinity of the sinking, many people changed their opinions and it was believed that the loss of the vessel was probably caused by her striking one of 35 mines laid by the German raider *Wolf* on the night of 27/28 August, 1917.

The *Wolf* also accounted for at least three other vessels in New Zealand waters, the *Wairuna* and *Winslow* were captured and sunk at the Kermadek Islands and the *Wimmera* struck a mine off the northern coast of the North Island. Under the command of Kurt Nerger this commerce raider sank over 140,000 tonnes of allied shipping in her fourteen months at sea.

German commmerce raiders were active around the New Zealand coast in both world wars and the country also had the distinction of holding prisoner the captain of one that never quite made it to our shores. Count Felix von Luckner commanded the armed barque *Seeadler* (Sea Eagle) and was responsible for the capture of no less than fourteen allied ships during a six month period in 1917.

When the *Seeadler* was wrecked at Mopelia atoll, in the Tuamotus, Luckner and a group of his men made one of the epic open boat voyages of all time, sailing from Mopelia to Wakaya Island in Fiji before being captured and transferred to New Zealand.

Nine weeks after being interned on Motuihe Island in the Hauraki Gulf he and a few fellow prisoners escaped in the commandant's launch, captured a scow and sailed off into the Pacific.

His freedom only lasted eight days before he was recaptured but he had, by then, written another page into New Zealand's history.

During World War II the raiders *Komet* and *Orion* were responsible for the sinking of several ships off our coasts, including the passenger liners *Rangitane* (see chapter one) and the *Niagara* (see chapter four).

The *Port Kembla* was built in 1910 for the Port Line and was a single screw steamer of 4,700 tons gross. At a little over 120m long she was one of the larger ships to be sunk off the New Zealand coast. On her last voyage she was bound from Melbourne to London via Wellington with a cargo of frozen meat, tallow, wool and lead. Twelve hundred tons of lead – and it is this lead that makes a salvage attempt so worthwhile. At 1995 prices lead was worth approximately NZ$1,000 per tonne so in total there is about NZ$1,200,000 worth of 'treasure' at the bottom of the sea off Cape Farewell.

Probably due to the depth of water over the wreck, over 100 metres, no thoughts were given to the early salvage of the *Port Kembla's* valuable cargo and it was not until 1952 that a British salvage company made a determined effort to locate the wreck. The attempt was abandoned when it was considered unlikely that the value of the lead, buried under three and a half thousand tonnes of perishable cargo would recompense the company for the effort of raising it.

The *Port Kembla* again sank into obscurity until, in the mid-1970s a Nelson based company, Nautilus Marine, became interested and, after a lengthy search, believed that they had pinpointed the wreckage on the sea floor with the aid of an echo-sounder in 1977. In consequence of this Nautilus Marine took out salvage rights on the wreck.

A special salvage vessel, the *Little Mermaid* was built in 1978 and was intended to be used on the *Port Kembla* before going on to serve the New Zealand oil and offshore construction industry.

By the time the *Little Mermaid* was ready for the salvage attempt it was discovered that, although she had a diving bell and recompression chamber on board, she was unsuitable for the task of a major salvage operation at the depth at which the *Port Kembla* lay. She was a small vessel, not specifically designed for deep wreck salvage and was instead used for more mundane commercial diving work.

The wreck site however had been located during the initial exploratory work and shows up well on an echo-sounder trace taken at the time, with proof of a wreck, in the form of a piece of iron and copper pipe and part of a ships rail, being hauled to the surface by a grapple. With the position known it is only a matter of time before someone descends to the wreck to investigate the feasibility of recovering the valuable cargo. An alternative, of course, would be to use an ROV (remote operated vehicle) to inspect the wreck first on video so that the practicalities of a major salvage effort could be assessed.

The depth at which the wreck lies will have protected the vessel to a certain extent from the ravages of the sea. Although there are probably quite strong bottom currents in the area there will be no surge or swell to strain and eventually destroy her form. It will only be time and corrosion that will cause her to collapse and, after less than eighty years, she could still be in reasonable condition. If so and if she has not sunk too deeply into the silt of the sea floor it would be interesting to inspect the explosion damage to the bow and to determine finally whether she sank because of internal sabotage or because she struck a mine. An internal explosion would cause jagged edges of the hole blown in her side to protrude outwards; with a mine the jagged edges would point inwards.

An interesting point about the salvage is that during the building of the *Little Mermaid* there was a lot of speculation as to whether the cargo of wool carried by the *Port Kembla* was worth salvaging as well. On the face of it this sounds rather like wishful thinking but in fact tests made on wool had shown that it could stand up to submersion in sea water for a remarkably long time, particularly when in compressed bales; the outside of the bales would certainly have deteriorated but how about the wool towards the centre?

To further strengthen this point was the fact that in October 1964 it was reported that a cargo of wool on the sunken United States freighter *Oregon*, which had been under water for twenty three years, was about to be salvaged. Divers had inspected the cargo and came to the conclusion that most of the wool was still usable and that the estimated value was £2,000,000 – and that was over thirty years ago!

Unfortunately, follow-up reports on this salvage venture do not appear to have made the New Zealand newspapers although the New Zealand Wool Board later stated that the salvage attempt had been postponed. But it could be that the *Port Kembla's* cargo is worth considerably more than just the value of the lead.

In 1983-4 there were definite plans for a full scale assault to be launched on the *Port Kembla* by a New Zealander but this plan has not yet been put to the test. There have also been several other rumours of intended salvage but whoever does attempt to raise the 1,200 tonnes of lead is going to need considerable financial and technical backing to have any chance of success. Good luck to them.

CHAPTER THREE

WAIRARAPA

A few days after the disaster the remains of the Union Steamship Company's ss *Wairarapa* are still partly above water. (Author's collection).

Many people have dived the wreck of the Union Steamship Company's *Wairarapa* and on many fine weekends in the Hauraki Gulf there is a dive boat of some kind anchored over her crumbling skeleton, but few of these people realise that there is treasure on this vessel. Exactly how much is anybody's guess but a conservative estimate would put the value at a quarter of a million dollars and it could well be much more.

The ss *Wairarapa* was built in Scotland in 1882 and was immediately brought to New Zealand as a cargo and passenger steamer for the trans-Tasman run. She served this and the New Zealand coastal route successfully for the next twelve years, earning a name for herself as a fast, comfortable vessel with a reputation for being reliable and keeping to her schedule. Only once did serious trouble occur when she caught fire off Gisborne in 1885, but no lives were lost and the fire was brought under control by the crew after several hours of strenuous effort. The captain and crew were commended by the Union Company for the way in which they handled the emergency and, after repairs to the ship she was put back into service.

In 1890 Captain John McIntosh took command of the *Wairarapa*. He was an experienced man who had been with the Union Company for about fifteen years and during the next four years became known as a careful, rather conservative man. A strict disciplinarian, he was popular with passengers and respected by the crew. On the night of 28/29 October, 1894 he lost his ship and his life in a disaster that should never have happened and has never been fully explained since.

On October 24 the *Wairarapa* had left Sydney, bound for Auckland with a full complement of passengers and a general cargo that included sixteen horses. There were over 250 people on board but less than half of them were destined to reach Auckland alive after what turned out to be the second or third worst maritime disaster in the history of New Zealand.

After an uneventful passage across the Tasman Captain McIntosh altered course at North Cape to steam down the east coast of the North Island towards Auckland. At that time fog came down thickly and it was the last land seen by the officers that day. A course change was again made when the captain thought that he was abreast of the Poor Knights Islands, this should have taken him into the Hauraki Gulf but what he did not know was that a combination of current and tide was driving his ship far to the east of his intended track. At eight minutes past midnight on 29 October, 1894, after being in fog for some twelve hours, the *Wairarapa* slammed into a 200 metre cliff near Miners Head on the northwestern end of Great Barrier Island.

Captain McIntosh, against the advice of his officers, had never during that twelve hours sounded the foghorn, taken soundings as instructed in the standing orders of the Union Steamship Company* or, most important of all, slowed his ship down. When she hit the cliff she was steaming full ahead at about thirteen knots.

The night was dark, foggy and with a considerable swell running although there was little wind, and when the *Wairarapa* struck, Captain McIntosh immediately ordered the engines to be put full speed astern. It appears that this had little effect which, for the sake of the 125 survivors is just as well. The vessel was badly holed below the waterline and had she managed to drag herself astern with her propellers she would almost certainly have sunk quickly in deep water; as it was she took a severe list to port, catapulting people, horses and loose gear over the side and rendering the starboard boats useless.

Waves swept across the decks and passengers streaming up from their cabins were plucked from their footing and hurled into the sea. Two of the three lifeboats on the port side were launched by the third and fourth officers and did valuable rescue work even though one of them was badly damaged. They were both finally swept out of the bay by the current and landed some distance down the coast.

After giving the order to go full astern and then for the engine to be stopped the captain, standing on the bridge, gave the order to lower the boats. That order, unbelievably, seems to have been the last he gave; he remained on the bridge for the next three hours and did absolutely nothing until, sometime after three in the morning, the bridge structure was washed overboard carrying the captain and several passengers with it. Few of these people lived and according to one of them the last words uttered by the captain were ". . . the last watch".

During these three hours of chaos the chief and second officers took refuge in the fore-rigging and appear to have done nothing. The second officer was an elderly man and maybe one can be charitable and say that he was unable to do anything, but the Chief Officer seemed to have no valid excuse for not taking control of the situation in the absence of his captain. In fact his excuse was that he was suffering from cramp, which would seem pretty feeble considering what was going on all around him and what the less fortunate passenger were suffering.

The other disturbing fact is that a far higher proportion of the crew survived the ordeal than did the passengers, the officers particularly seeming to have fared better than anyone. Out of thirteen officers only two lost their lives – the captain

---

*By sounding the foghorn the officers would almost certainly have heard an echo from the 200 metre sheer wall in front of them and by taking regular soundings a captain could ascertain when the sea floor was shelving up towards land. If this happened the ship would normally be slowed down and turned aside or stopped until the fog lifted.

and the chief steward.

With the three senior officers taking no active part in the proceedings and the two juniors out in the boats the remaining crew and passengers , lacking any sort of leadership, considered it to be every man for himself and, although there were many brave and selfless acts that night, there was also cowardice and selfishness. There were many instances where men were warmly dressed and could have given up some of their clothing to the women dressed only in a shift or nightdress. The women in particular seem to have shown great fortitude and all three stewardesses, not one of whom survived, were eulogised in the press for months afterwards.

When daylight came a rope was taken ashore by one of the stewards, a difficult task that almost cost him his life, and the remaining passengers and crew started to leave the stricken ship.

Nothing was easy at Miners Head, the cliffs went straight down into the sea

With nothing onto which to tie the life line survivors from the *Wairarapa*, with their bare feet on the sharp rocks, are forced to hold it tight themselves. (Auckland Institute & Museum).

and, apart from a few rocky ledges, there was nowhere to stand. Having managed to get the rope ashore there was nothing to which to attach it and men, standing on the sharp rocks in their bare feet, had to hold it while people crossed from the ship. In these circumstances it is no wonder that two girls fell from the rope and were drowned, but the remainder were safely taken ashore where they had to huddle for a further twelve hours with nothing to sustain them but a few oranges washed ashore from the wreck.

Meanwhile, the third mate had alerted the local settlers and, together with Maori from the Ngapuhi tribe, they set out to the rescue, doing valiant work and the Maori afterwards putting up and feeding 125 extra people for a further two days (for which it would appear that they were rather poorly recompensed by the Union Steamship Company).

Because of the remoteness of Great Barrier Island the news of the tragedy did not reach the mainland until the *Argyle* called three days later on her weekly trip. On her arrival days were spent recovering the bodies of the drowned and either interring them on the island or shipping them back to Auckland for burial. Of the approximately 130 who lost their lives about forty bodies were never found.

Confusion reigned as to exactly who had died in the wreck; all the records on board had been lost and with the service run by the *Wairarapa* passengers could pay their fares directly to the purser on sailing day, so there was no complete passenger-list ashore.

The official list of the dead named 125 persons but almost certainly more than these died that night on Great Barrier Island. There are so many discrepancies in all the records that it is impossible to come to an accurate conclusion, but taking everything into account and reading between the lines there must have been at least 130 deaths and probably several more.

Salvage of the vessel started almost as soon as it had been wrecked and the first priority was to recover the mails. Not all were recovered but not for the want of trying and when everything had been done in that direction the company turned it's attention to trying to save some of the cargo and stores. Little was recovered and it was not long before they cut their losses and cancelled the salvage attempt when the vessel started to break up – although she was still partly above water at this stage. The locals, too, got into the act and there are several stories of men reaching through portholes to see what they could find.

By the time somebody else was interested in salvage it was 1923 and the *Wairarapa* was completely submerged. The company concerned was represented at the site by William Vear and Jock McKinnon, both experienced hard-hat divers, and their intentions were to remove all the non-ferrous metals from the wreck to sell as scrap. The manganese-bronze propeller, five or six tonnes of brass tubing from the condenser, copper and lead piping and brass fittings were all lifted in the next few weeks. They also found and recovered an undisclosed number of lead pigs from the cargo and searched unsuccessfully for the ship's safe.

Another thirty four years passed before further interest was shown in the remains of the *Wairarapa*. Les Subritzki led a group of aqualung divers to the site in 1957 and came away with hundreds of kilograms of brass, copper and lead fittings, but little of anything other than scrap or souvenir value. He continued to dive the wreck sporadically for many years and in 1969 found the compass in almost perfect condition but little that could be described as treasure.

So why is the *Wairarapa* included in a book of treasure wrecks? She was not carrying bullion and, apart from forty-eight pigs of lead and a few tin ingots on her manifest, was carrying little in her holds that would have survived the years underwater. Fruit, timber, cloth, sewing machines and foodstuffs comprised the majority of the cargo.

One clue to hidden wealth is the mention of the ship's gold safe – but it could be a very misleading clue. This safe was located below the saloon stairs and as far as anyone knows it has never been found. As far as any records reveal, it had nothing in it but this may not have been the case. It is known that several gold miners were travelling on the ship and who knows whether they had struck it rich in Australia and possibly decided to have their wealth locked away in the safe? It is unlikely that there was anything of great value in it as the purser, who survived the wreck, would almost certainly have mentioned it.

Rumour has it that the safe was taken off the vessel at the time of the disaster but this is not borne out by any of the testimony at the Court of Enquiry and the passengers and crew, seeing a safe taking up valuable space in one of the only two lifeboats to leave the stricken vessel, would have been sure to have let their feelings be known.

There is a report that the purser's safe was recovered by the salvage team in 1923 but this was almost certainly a small safe – really an elaborate cash box - that was kept in the purser's cabin and not the so called 'Gold Safe'. What was in the purser's safe history does not relate but obviously it was not a great deal, if anything at all, or the divers would have spoken about the contents or else kept very quiet about finding the safe.

The main gold safe still lies on the sea floor at Miners Head and will probably be found one day although the finder could be very disappointed because it is unlikely that much of the treasure lies within.

Maybe the following letter will explain the form of the treasure still on the *Wairarapa*; written on the day after the news broke about the tragedy it is an amazing example of greed disregarding, as it does, the fate of the passenger concerned. At this time the confusion was so great that no one knew for certain who had survived and who had drowned. It was addressed to the Union Steamship Company: "Dear Sir, I want you to try by all means to recover Mrs Stewart's luggage from the wreck of the *Wairarapa*. Mrs Stewart booked by Cooks and occupied No. 15 berth. Had in hold one large travelling trunk – French make marked C.S. large leather straps and canvas cover. Had in berth black handbag containing 30 sovereigns gold watch on jet chain. Please communicate with me should any of the above be recovered."

Mrs Stewart died on 29 October, 1894 and her possessions were certainly not recovered in the early days of salvage – no doubt much to the chagrin of the letter writer.

Several letters still in existence mirror the sentiments of that shown above – although not quite so callously. They frequently mention money lost on the wreck by those who did not make it to shore and, although some of this was certainly on the persons of those who drowned, the passengers were asleep at the time of the wreck and most of them rushed on deck to find out what had happened only to discover that they could not get back to their cabins once the vessel had listed to port. Most of their money and personal possessions went down with the ship.

At a conservative estimate the money lost would be at least 1,000 gold coins and also many articles of jewellery. At today's prices this would be worth an absolute minimum of $500,000 – well worth searching for even at our inflated costs of diving and hiring boats.

Some years ago Wade Doak wrote an article for *Dive* magazine in which he described a dive on the *Wairarapa* with, among other people, Kelly Tarlton. Tarlton surfaced after the dive with an 18ct gold wedding ring. The last paragraph of the article told of a later dive on the wreck when they recovered from the baggage room in the bows of the ship, cufflinks, a silver gravy boat, a diamond ring with two rubies, a gold watch chain and a cameo. This was only the start of the finds on this wreck but certainly not the finish.

Since the late 1960s several gold coins, watches and watch chains have been found but the surface has only been scratched. For every sovereign recovered there must be at least ten still on the wreck and in the sand alongside the rocky cliffs there must be many more that were on the persons of those who tried so desperately to get ashore in the heavy swell.

Yes, there is a great deal of gold still on or near the *Wairarapa* but it is not easy to find and will never all be found. It is scattered throughout the ship and along a 400m stretch of the shore and involves a lot of hard work to uncover even one coin; but the rewards are high and worth the effort for anyone who is prepared to exert himself – but, permission should be obtained from the Historic Places Trust or whoever is the current holder of the salvage rights!

CHAPTER FOUR

NIAGARA

The bullion Carrier RMS *Niagara* in happier days. (G.H. Edwards collection –
Alexander Turnbull Library).

Shortly after the end of World War I the *Niagara* made headlines in New Zealand. She was suspected of being instrumental in bringing an influenza epidemic to our shores when she berthed in Auckland on 12 October, 1918. Health authorities should never have cleared the vessel as she had over one hundred cases of the fatal disease on board, but she was also carrying the Prime Minister, Mr. W.F. Massey and the Minister of Finance, Sir Joseph Ward. It was obviously deemed more important to allow these people to land than to place the ship in quarantine – political expediency, it would seem, can circumvent the health laws.

Whether the *Niagara* was the culprit or not has never been proved but the epidemic took a heavy toll in New Zealand. Before it had run its course more than five thousand people had died (some put the figure as high as seven thousand) and countless thousands had been afflicted by the deadly virus.

The *Niagara* was a triple-screw steamer of 13,415 tons gross, built in Scotland in 1913, and her part in the influenza epidemic was not to be the last time that she made sensational headlines. On June 18, 1940, she sailed from Auckland bound for Suva and Vancouver with 146 passengers and 203 crew. Stowed in her holds was a large cargo of small-arms ammunition destined for the war in Europe, and in her strong room was eight tonnes of gold from South Africa owned by the Bank of England and worth, at the time, £2½ million (in Kurt Weyher's book *The Black Raider* this figure is put at £5,000,000).

The weather was fine and clear as the *Niagara* steamed out of Auckland Harbour on the first leg of her voyage, but Captain Martin was not a happy man. He knew the value of his cargo to the allied war effort and was aware that German raiders were operating in the Pacific – but even he must have been shocked by the speed with which disaster overtook him.

At 3.40am on 19 June, 1940, only a few hours after sailing, and while she was between Bream Head and Mokohinau Island, the *Niagara* struck and detonated a mine laid on the 13 or 14 June by the German raider *Orion*. A violent explosion threw people from their bunks but, although a few of the passengers were slightly injured, there was no panic and within twenty minutes most were in the lifeboats. At 5.32am the vessel sank in position 35°56'S latitude, 174°54'E longitude and in nearly seventy fathoms of water. Although no lives were lost in the accident, the loss to the allied cause was incalculable.

Almost six months later salvage operations were started to remove the gold bullion from her strong room, but the difficulties were enormous. The wreck lay in about one hundred and thirty metres of water, said at the time to be the deepest salvage ever attempted. With war time restrictions the salvors had to make do with a thirty-eight-year-old ship that had been abandoned years before, as their salvage tender. The *Claymore* was not really suitable for the task but there was nothing else available and on 15 December, 1940 operations commenced to locate the wreck. Six weeks later, on 2 February, 1941 they found her.

The gold was in two hundred and ninety five wooden boxes with two ingots in each box, and was located in the strongroom, virtually in the centre of the vessel. Using a one-man diving bell chief diver Johnstone and his brother took turns in descending to the wreck to lay charges and blast away the ship's hull until the strongroom could be reached. It was slow, dangerous work and necessitated the diver below giving instructions over the telephone to the grab operator on the deck of the *Claymore*. This man, using the eyes of the diver, delicately laid the charges in the positions he was told. When the diver had been raised to the surface and the charge detonated, he then picked up any junk that was blocking further operations and dropped it clear of the wreck.

Danger to the divers came not only from the inherent dangers of working 130

Survivors from the *Niagara* head for the rescue ship after abandoning the stricken liner. (Alexander Turnbull Library).

metres below the surface but also from the grab itself which tended to foul the safety lines of the bell. On several occasions German mines came close to blowing up chief diver Johnstone and the *Claymore*. In a booklet entitled *Niagara Gold* written by R.J. Dunn and published by A.H. & A.W. Reed in 1942, the author describes one of these near misses:

"As the bell was in the process of hoisting, a wire rope scraped the side. Although fouled the bell swung clear at about 15 feet, leaving a big query mark in the mind of the diver, who, peering through the window, had scanned the foreign wire. The mystery was solved after lunch, when, on the anchor being hauled up before recommencing sweeping operations, a mass of green sea growth was brought to the surface. Upon a few more yards of cable being hoisted aboard, the ugly shape of a mine, complete with holding shackle and horns protruding five inches, was revealed. Tangled with the cable chain, it scraped the Claymore's side.

"Faced with such deadly peril, Captain Williams gave instructions to lower away slowly, and after a dress suit diver had been sent down to investigate the mine, it was decided to slip the moorings and report the discovery to the Naval authorities.

"Escorted by a minesweeper, the Claymore returned to the spot where the mine had been buoyed off alongside one of the permanent moorings. So great was the danger that, with the exception of Captain Williams, diver Johnstone, two men on the diver's pump and two attendants, the Claymore's crew, together with the ship's papers, were transferred to the minesweeper. Once the ship had been abandoned, diver Johnstone again went down in diving dress and shackled the light sweep wire provided by the minesweeper on to the mine itself. While doing this he noticed to his concern that the holding wire of the mine was wrapped round the Claymore's mooring wire, of which it had already cut two strands.

"Freed by the diver, the mine shot up the mooring wire to within two feet of the Claymore's side, carrying Mr. Johnstone, whose lifeline was enmeshed with the horns, up with it. There he remained, clutching two horns and with the top of his helmet touching the Claymore's bottom. Captain Williams then gave word to the minesweeper to pull on the wire so that the mine was taken clear of the ship. This operation, ticklish in the extreme, was nearing completion when the wire broke, the mine shooting to the surface within ten feet of the Claymore's bows. After seven nerve-wracking hours, it was finally riddled with machine-gun bullets and sunk."

The salvage company, United Salvage Pty. Ltd. of Melbourne, was represented on the site by Captain J.P. Williams who was highly commended for his handling of the operation. Chief diver Johnstone paid tribute in his diary to the superb leadership of this man.

Piece by piece the wrecked hull of the *Niagara* was blasted and wrenched away until on 13 October, 1941, over eight months since locating the vessel, the grab dipped into the shattered strongroom and deposited on the deck of the *Claymore* two shining gold bars. The salvage crew were understandably jubilant, they had succeeded in one of the most difficult salvage operations ever undertaken, and from that time on the work tempo increased.

Over the next seven weeks a total of five hundred and fifty five gold bars were recovered, leaving only thirty five still in the wreck but in such a position as to make it uneconomic to attempt their salvage. Two million three hundred and seventy nine thousand pounds worth of gold had been raised before a halt was called to the operations on 8 December, 1941, the day after America belatedly entered the war.

For twelve years after the initial salvage effort the remains of the *Niagara* were left undisturbed; but the value of gold was increasing and in 1953 another salvage company, Risdon Beasley Ltd. of Southhampton, made a second bid for the remaining bullion. After considerable effort and expense they succeeded in raising thirty of the thirty five bars still in the vessel before abandoning the task. They considered that the remaining five bars were in no position to be raised without the venture becoming unprofitable.

Of these five bars three remain in the strongroom where a grab could not reach them and the other two accidentally fell from the grab during the first salvage operation and apparently disappeared into the depths of the engine room from where it was impossible to recover them.

Some people are still interested in the *Niagara* and her remaining five gold bars and as recently as 1973 a company, Blue Vein Shipping Corporation Ltd., took out the salvage rights on her but presumably never proceeded further with their planning.

In the late 1970s several New Zealanders became involved in experimenting with deep diving using mixed gasses and at least two of these intended to put their knowledge to the test by a bounce dive on the *Niagara* before their plans were put paid to by the unfortunate death of one of their number.

Mixed gas diving requires the wearing of two tanks, one containing compressed air and the other the gas mixture. When the late diver was ascending after a deep dive off the Poor Knights Islands he had to change from the mixture back to air at a depth of 50 metres before continuing his ascent. It is believed that the regulator on his air tank had become tangled in his back-pack harness and that he tried to make a rapid ascent using the gas mixture and that he died from an embolism on reaching the surface.

Experimenting with mixed gas diving is an extremely dangerous business and although the diver concerned did not die as a direct result of breathing the wrong mixture the other diver very nearly died for this reason on an earlier dive. At one hundred metres off Mana Island he started hallucinating badly and talks about seeing the faces of people he had not seen since his childhood, he felt sick and disorientated and only by a superhuman effort of will power managed

Artifacts from the *Niagara* on display at the Museum of Shipwrecks in Waitangi. (Kelly Tarlton).

to pull himself back up the shot-line. When he reached eighty metres the symptoms disappeared and he was able to surface normally.

In the late 1980s Keith Gordon of SeaROV Services sent a remote operated vehicle (ROV) down to the *Niagara* and videotaped the wreck, finding it still to be intact apart from the depredations made on the hull by the earlier salvage operations. The team he was leading were surprised to learn that the depth of the sea floor on the site was 118 metres, not the originally reported 133 metres. The only logical explanation of this anomaly is that, as reputedly the deepest ever salvage attempt at the time, it was used as propaganda to counter the slightly shallower salvage of the *Egypt* at 120 metres, carried out by the Italians in 1931. At the time of the salvage of the *Niagara* the Italians were the enemy!

The ROV is an extremely accurate instrument and it is unlikely that the depth readings shown on the videotape are more than a metre or so out – and the range of the tide would not account for the difference between 118 and 133 metres when the maximum variation in the area is only about three metres.

The *Niagara* still holds immense fascination for divers and dives on her using mixed gas apparatus are still talked about by a few but, so far, nobody has attempted this. With the price of gold rising as it has since 1940 the five remaining bars are a tempting prize worth hundreds of thousands of dollars and in the not too distant future someone will probably go after them, but it is deep treacherous water and it is as likely that they will lose their lives as find any of the bullion. By now it will be covered in silt and debris and without an extremely dangerous entry into, and search of, the engine room there are only three bars to recover.

An alternative method would be to attempt the recovery of the gold using only robot devices but with the cost of this type of venture it is probable that the remaining bullion would not cover the cost of the undertaking.

CHAPTER FIVE

GENERAL GRANT

An artist's impression of the final moments of the full-rigged ship *General Grant*.
(Author's collection).

Because of modern attempts to locate the wreck of the elusive *General Grant* it is probably the best known of the New Zealand treasure wrecks, although it is certainly the most remote.

Ever since the vessel was wrecked in 1866 at the inhospitable Auckland Islands, about three hundred kilometres south of New Zealand, there have been successive attempts to find the gold she is known to have been carrying, all of them so far without the slightest success.

The full-rigged ship *General Grant* sank on 14 May, 1866 after being becalmed and washed into the cliffs of the forbidding Auckland Islands. She ended her days in an enormous cave where the rising tide is said to have forced the masts against the roof and then through the bottom of the ship. Of the eighty three people on board only fifteen made it to shore where ten of them were destined to spend the next eighteen months. Of the other five one died on the islands and four were lost whilst trying to get help in a small boat. The ten survivors, including one woman, were finally picked up by a whaler after spending a year and a half of privation and misery, barely managing to stay alive.

On board the *General Grant* when she sank were 2,576 ounces of gold and many of the passengers were miners returning to England with, as the rumours tell us, their fortunes in their money belts. At 1995 prices the known gold would be worth about $NZ1.5 million and there could be much more.

Some of the earliest attempts to find the *General Grant's* gold were made shortly after the castaways had been rescued and were accompanied by some of the survivors. The first, in 1868, was abandoned when the weather was of such severity that the treasure hunters could not enter the cave in which the ship sank. The second, in 1870, was called off when six men lost their lives while searching for the cave in an open boat – one of those who died was David Ashworth who had already survived the eighteen month ordeal on the island. The third attempt, in 1876 and with another survivor, Cornelius Drew, on board, tried to approach the cave from the land but they were frustrated in their efforts by the cliffs and the general difficulties of this method. Finding the correct cave from above must have been almost impossible when he had only ever seen it from the sea eight years before.

In 1877 a further attempt was made but for some reason the diver never went below even though the weather was perfect and they had found what they thought was the right cave.

Thirty five years passed before someone again set up a salvage operation but this never got as far as leaving New Zealand and it was not until 1915/16 that a diver again visited the Auckland Islands. This time he made several descents but was unable to find the wreck and the salvors eventually had to call it a day when they ran out of money.

Around this period stories started circulating about the nine tons of spelter – a zinc alloy – included on the *General Grant's* manifest. It was rumoured that this was, in fact, really gold. The story seems to have originated either from a 1913/14 copy of *Chambers Journal* or from an Australian who claimed that he had in his possession notes written by William Sanguilly, a survivor of the wrecking, stating that the captain had instructed him to mark a special consignment as 'spelter' to decieve ex-convicts and possible pirates among the crew and passengers, but that actually the 'spelter' was gold valued at £120,000 – a fortune in those days.

This story seems to re-appear everytime there is interest shown in the *General Grant* but there seems to be little substance in it and no solid evidence has ever come to light. It would seem to be incredible that there is no verification of the loss of nine tons of gold, either from the shipper or from those who should have received it. Another intriguing question is why would the shippers say that some of the gold was 'spelter' when the 2576 ounces was openly declared as gold on

The forbidding cliffs of the Auckland Islands, where the *General Grant* sank, with the Grattan wreck (presumably the *Anjou*) in the cave piercing the point. (John Dearling).

the manifest? This was worth a lot of money in 1866 and would also have been a temptation to 'pirates and ex-convicts'. Could this just be a rumour put about by potential salvors trying to obtain investment for the venture, or are there really notes from William Sanquilly – and if so where are they?

In the mid-1950s several plans were laid but most never got further than the planning stage. One concern consisting of Australians and Englishmen did set out three times from Scotland, however. The first time a storm damaged the salvage vessel so badly that they had to put back to port, in the other two attempts they were frustrated by being shipwrecked themselves, once in the Red Sea and once on the coast of Portuguese Timor – there are no records indicating that they tried a fourth time!

In 1970 scuba divers visited the Auckland Islands for the first time with the intention of searching for the wreck but with little success. They did find an anchor but this was too small to have come from the *General Grant*, it could however have come from a vessel belonging to one of the earlier salvage attempts as one of these had recorded having lost an anchor outside a cave answering to the survivors descriptions. The cave was searched thoroughly but no sign of a wreck was found. Could this be a clue to the whereabouts of the *General Grant*? It is possible that she was washed out of the cave after the crew had left and sank somewhere close by.

Had they found the wreck the divers intention was to return the following year to unearth the gold but as their search was fruitless they returned to the mainland.

At this time people started believing that there was more of a mystery surrounding the position of the remains of the *General Grant* and the whereabouts of the treasure than had previously been thought and stories of skulduggery among the crew started surfacing.

Had the crew in fact reported the position of the wreck incorrectly so that they themselves could return and collect the gold? Had an American expedition, soon after the rescue of the survivors, already made a successful voyage to the Auckland Islands? A few of the rescued crewmen had been to the United States within a year of the end of their ordeal and an American attempt could have been mounted at this time.

Malcolm Blair, one of the divers who was on several later expeditions and has done a great deal of research into the wreck, believes that the crew could not possibly have known the location of the cave anyway as they were wrecked at night and saw the area only briefly from the sea, under highly unfavourable conditions, until after they had been rescued eighteen months later. Even people who know the coast well can be fooled nowadays if the weather changes, and with the dozens of similar caves the crew would be hard pressed to unerringly pick the right one.

All this is academic however and did not in the slightest influence the thinking of the next treasure hunter to come on the scene.

In the early months of 1974 newspapers reported that a Royal Navy Commander by the name of John Grattan, said to be one of the world's leading salvage divers, was trying to raise $30,000 to finance an expedition to the Auckland Islands where he believed he could recover $4,000,000 in gold from the remains of the *General Grant.*

The supposed value of the gold waiting to be salvaged fluctuated wildly over the months and by the time Commander Grattan's team left Dunedin heading south on 13 January, 1975, it appears to have sunk to an all-time low at $300,000.

After an extensive search of the western coastline of the main island in the Auckland group, New Zealand diver John Dearling came across a part of a rudder in an area that could have fitted the description given by the survivors. As soon as this discovery was known on board the dive tender Malcolm Blair and Kelly Tarlton dived and found a pile of wreckage including several anchors and the top of a bell, but this, unfortunately, had no identification on it. However, a shipwreck had definitely been located.

On 18 January newspapers published a telegram from Mr. G.P. O'Farrell, the man financing the expedition, which read in part: *"Today at 4.10pm, after four days diving, the team are elated having located a wreck giving the strongest*

A diver inspects an anchor on the Grattan wreck site. (Kelly Tarlton).

indications of being the ill-fated clipper, the General Grant".

Three days later a further telegram stated that the *General Grant* had been found ". . . with all reasonable certainty."

From this time on the value of the treasure on the vessel started to rise and on 23 January was reported as $500,000. Commander Grattan's team of divers had recovered several artifacts but they had still not found anything to positively identify the wreck – and they had certainly found no gold!

On returning to New Zealand most of the team were convinced that they had found the *General Grant* and, although no bullion had been located, a further trip was planned for January 1976 when heavy lifting gear would be used to remove the large rocks covering the area – the gold should be underneath.

Towards the end of 1975 Commander Grattan suffered setbacks, not least of which was that Gerald O'Farrell, who had been intending to finance the second expedition, had been declared bankrupt. John Grattan however was undaunted and looked elsewhere for the money he needed, eventually funding the trip from a variety of sources including a deal with the New Zealand Broadcasting Corporation for the film rights.

During this time Kelly Tarlton was having second thoughts about the identity of the wreckage that had been found and was on several occasions reported as saying he believed it was from the French barque *Anjou* that had sunk at the Auckland Islands in 1905. There was too much iron on the site, he said, for it to have been the *General Grant.* There were also several other factors that did not fit in with the research he had done on the vessel. Some of the pieces that had been recovered had metric threads and this did not conform with an American-built ship. Convinced that the expedition would be wasting its time Tarlton declined to go south again and concentrated instead on his salvage of the *Tasmania* jewellery.

Also in late 1975 the alleged value of the *General Grant's* treasure leapt upwards most dramatically and was reported as being as high as $50,000,000. The spelter question had surfaced again and John Grattan believed that apart from the 2576oz of gold known to be on the vessel the nine tons marked 'spelter' was also in fact gold. Nine tons of gold would be worth a vast amount of money.

When the second Grattan expedition left New Zealand at the beginning of January 1976 they took with them a reporter from the *Observer* in London and, in a separate boat, a television film crew. What they did not know was that another group had stolen a march on them and had left for the Auckland Islands a few days earlier. The *Atlantis* was a fishing boat with at least two divers on board. On January 8, the two boats met over the wreck site and there were harsh words and high tempers all round. Commander Grattan on the *Acheron* eventually chased the 'pirates' away however, and they were not seen again by his party. The *Atlantis* arrived back at Bluff on 12 January and was soon in trouble with the Marine Department for leaving New Zealand without their authority and without permits to visit the Auckland Islands.

Meanwhile, the *Acheron's* divers were working hard on removing the rocks off the wreck site and being continually frustrated by the weather. They did however clear a large area only to be confronted by sand – and they had no equipment on board to effectively remove this next challenge. Malcolm Blair, the only New Zealand diver on the second expedition, described in his diary what they were reduced to: *"The only method was to use a large drum, a bucket and a shovel. Using lifting bags was too slow. The cost of the expedition was $5,000 per diving day and down there putting sand into a bucket with a shovel seemed unreal".*

And 'unreal' it was . Hopes had started out high but towards the end of January time and money had run out and the *Acheron* returned to Dunedin with no sign of the treasure. They had been beaten principally by the weather but also through the lack of efficient sand moving equipment – or was it that they were on the wrong wreck? Once again a small part of a bell had been found, this time a section of the bottom, and on this was part of an inscription that looks like the base curl of a letter 'J', or possibly a figure 3, 5 or 9. These do not appear in the

Plaster cast of a small brass plate recovered from the Grattan wreck site virtually proving that the wreck is that of the Nantes built *Anjou*. (Steve Locker-Lampson).

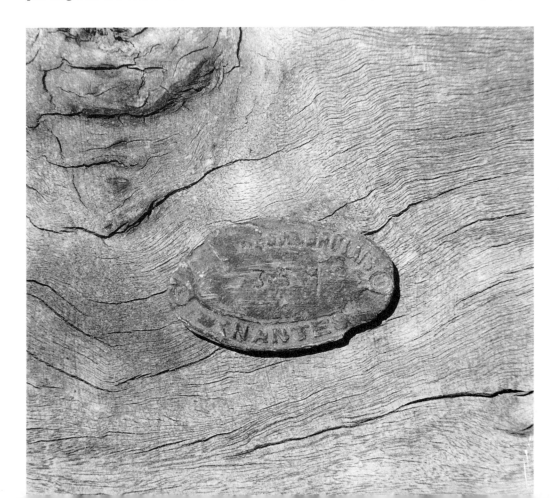

General Grant's name or date of building but it is just possible that it could have come from another wreck in the area, that of the French, steel barque named *Anjou*, built in 1899 and wrecked in 1905.

John Grattan's 1976 expedition is the last he has made to the *General Grant* site to date. Several other trips have been planned including a further one on the *Atlantis* that was going to search an area pointed out by a clairvoyant on the previous, 'pirate' trip. A Christchurch property developer, Brooke McKenzie and fisherman John Baxter tried to raise public money for an attempt in late 1976 and sailed for the Auckland Islands in April 1977, defying a Ministry of Transport ban on the vessel leaving port. They were later to sail back empty handed. On his return from the islands Mr McKenzie stated that he had located another wreck and was convinced that it was the *General Grant*. His divers had found a plate with the date 1862 on it as well as other artifacts but he was reported as saying that nothing had been removed from the wreck, just photographed. He planned a further trip to recover the bullion, he said, but as yet this has not occurred although it was still being planned as late as 1979 and rumour has it that this may still be in the wind.

A syndicate comprising seven divers on the dive tender *Little Mermaid* set out for the Auckland Islands in 1986 and again started excavations on the wreck discovered by Commander Grattan's crew.

During their exploration of this wreck a brass plate was discovered bearing an inscription, including the name of the French city of Nantes, that indicated to the syndicate members that they must, with 99% certainty, be on the site of the wreck of the French-built *Anjou* – definitely not a treasure wreck.

In growing anxiety they searched further along the western coast of the main island until they found another wreck which seemed to fit the vital statistics of the *General Grant*. On the site they found three anchors and two iron carronades and, over the next few days, used their pump to see if anything lay beneath the sand and shingle of the sea floor.

Somewhat to their surprise they started finding silver coins and before the weather forced them to leave the area sixty one half crowns and two copper coins had been recovered. The elation of the syndicate was high even though no gold had been found but their hopes were somewhat dashed when it was found that all the coins were dated before 1830.

The *General Grant* was wrecked in 1866 and it seems to be unlikely that the coins recovered were from her when the latest is dated thirty six years before the disaster – but, who can say for certain?

Those who discovered this latest wreck are understandably reluctant to disclose its exact position although it is known to be on the west coast of the main island. Most of them are, however, convinced that they have at last discovered the remains of the real *General Grant*.

Strangely enough this team also discovered a part of a bell, this time just the bottom rim. For three expeditions to have found three different pieces of bells, on two different wrecks is unusual in that none of these pieces definitely identify a particular vessel but the second piece, with the hint of the bottom curl of a letter or figure on it, would indicate that the Grattan wreck is probably that of the *Anjou* − particularly if it was from a figure 9, the last figure of the date of building.

The Southern Ocean Exploration syndicate divers on board the *Little Mermaid* with some of the recovered artifacts from the second wreck believed to be the *General Grant* and known as the half-crown wreck. (Malcolm Blair).

At the end of 1994 new reports were beginning to appear in the press regarding a syndicate seeking almost $4,000,000 through a public share issue for a further attempt on the *General Grant's* gold, this time to be again led by Commander John Grattan, with the 1977 expedition's John Baxter and Sydney private investigator Ashley Keith in the team. This expedition was intending to set forth in March 1995 and the value of the gold seems to have risen once again. In early January 1995 a press report stated that it could be worth ". . . up to $60,000,000 at today's prices", and on 25 January one of the syndicate was reported to have said that if the 'spelter' was really gold it would be worth about $250,000,000!

On 20 February, during a television interview with John Grattan, it was

Kelly Tarlton cleans *Elingamite* coins in his home-made electrolysis baths. (Kelly Tarlton).

Some of the *Elingamite* silver on display at the Museum of Shipwrecks on the *Tui* at Waitangi. (S.L-L)

A block of uncleaned *Elingamite* coins as most of them would have appeared underwater. (S.L-L)

Many of the half sovereigns recovered from the *Elingamite* by Kelly Tarlton (S.L-L)

Artist's impression of the last minutes of the ss *Tasmania.* (Museum of Shipwrecks, Waitangi).

Kelly Tarlton repositions his suction dredge over what he hopes is the *Tasmania's* "pay dirt". (Quentin Bennett).

The well known New Zealand treasure hunter, the late Kelly Tarlton, preparing to dive on the *Tasmania*. (Pat Ryan).

Richard Jones fins over a piece of *Tasmania's* rotting machinery. (Quentin Bennett).

An example of how difficult it can be to identify treasure – a gold pocket watch embedded in concretion. (S.L-L)

A gold watch from the *Tasmania* after cleaning. (S.L-L)

A few of the restored pocket watch cases from the *Tasmania.* (S.L-L)

A partially cleaned gold bracelet studded with diamonds and rubies from the *Tasmania.* (S.L-L)

Two beautiful charm bracelet bicycles on which the wheels still go round even after more than 60 years underwater. (S.L-L)

A selection of the many jewel encrusted rings that were recovered from the *Tasmania*. (S.L-L)

Just some of the *Tasmania's* magnificent jewellery. (Pat Ryan).

Battered copper sheathing and bronze pins found on the half-crown wreck prove that the vessel was constructed of wood. (John Dearling).

Nine silver half-crowns and two copper coins found on the half-crown wreck. (Malcolm Blair).

announced that the prospectus for the share float had been launched that day but that now the syndicate was seeking $5,000,000. Also that the *General Grant* treasure now included "170 mysterious packages", apparently owned by gold miners, having been given to the captain for safe keeping. It is known that there were "170 packages of passenger merchandise" on board but where the rumour of them being handed to the captain originated is rather obscure. There were only 83 people on the vessel when it was wrecked and only about twenty five of these were male passengers. Few of these are likely to have been gold miners and of those that were it is unlikely that they would have all struck it rich. Hard evidence for this type of claim seems to be singularly lacking.

Due to adverse criticism in the media by local experts the public became wary of the venture and the share float was wound up in late March 1995, and with their licence due to expire in September of that year it is unlikely that Commander Grattan's syndicate will visit the Auckland Islands again.

However, it is probable that a further expedition, by a different syndicate, will be launched during 1996. This group is believed to be intending to head for the 'half crown' wreck rather than that now almost universally believed to be the *Anjou*, as the 1995 John Grattan party were intending to excavate.

And so the mystery remains; has the *General Grant* been found and if so by which team? Is there $250,000,000 worth of gold still among her remains or just that shown on her manifest and worth around $1,500,000 at current rates but considerably more with its novelty and antiquity value taken into account? Or has every last ounce of gold already been removed by persons unknown? These questions and many more are still intriguing prospective salvors. With more advanced diving and salvage techniques being developed all the time it is likely that the *General Grant* will be found and excavated in the future and the gold recovered – if it is still there. Treasure of this sort is rarely allowed to rest undisturbed for very long!

CHAPTER SIX

TARARUA

Artist's impression of the plight of the *ss Tararua* (DeMaus collection – Alexander Turnbull Library).

A treasure wreck that was associated with great loss of life was the Union Steamship Company's ss *Tararua* while sailing from Port Chalmers to Hobart and Melbourne via Bluff during April 1881. In the early morning on 29 April she struck Waipapa Reef off a remote stretch of the Southland coast, some thirty kilometres east of Bluff. The impact destroyed the rudder and propeller leaving her helpless and at the mercy of the sea. On board at the time were one hundred and fifty one people, general cargo and several thousand pounds worth of silver.

Hard and fast on the reef the danger did not appear to be too great and when one of the passengers managed to swim ashore from a lifeboat the spirits of those on board must have been lifted to think that help was on the way. Unfortunately the heroic passenger, after finding a nearby runholder, despatched a message saying that all the remaining passengers were safe – which was true at the time – but neglecting to say that the situation was, in fact, critical. Because of this the *Hawea*, in Dunedin, was unhurried and loaded extra food, tow ropes and other equipment for what they thought would be a salvage operation of the *Tararua* herself. This delay in sailing meant that the *Hawea* did not arrive at the scene of the wreck until almost twenty four hours after the *Tararua* had gone aground, and by that time it was dark and nothing could be done until daylight.

When the first light of dawn broke over the scene watchers on the *Hawea* were horrified to see that the wreck had been smashed to pieces on the reef during the night. Flotsam and corpses littered the sea and although the *Hawea* searched for some hours she did not pick up even one living person from the water.

The full horror of the situation had become obvious to the passengers and crew on the crippled ship much earlier. After the initial impact the passengers seem to have panicked and it was not until they had been calmed down by the officers and crew that the latter were able to start doing something about the ship itself. Signal guns were fired, rockets sent up and flares burned but none of these attracted the attention of anyone in this remote part of the South Island. The lifeboats were swung outboard (one of which was instantly smashed by the heavy swell) but not used immediately. From all reports the crew worked in an efficient, organised manner under the direction of Captain Francis Garrard and, when everything possible was done the passengers were placed in the smoking room to await the time that they could leave the stricken vessel.

At first light Mr Maloney, the second officer, took a boat away from the ship to try to find a landing place only to be defeated by the breakers on the reef. Mr Lawrence, a passenger who had been taken in the boat because he was an excellent swimmer, then jumped overboard and managed, after a dangerous and gruelling swim across rocks, to reach the shore and alert a local runholder who, in turn, sent a messenger to the nearest telegraph office almost fifty kilometres away.

The second officer meanwhile, took his boat back to the *Tararua* and six passengers who volunteered to also try to get ashore through the surf were lowered into it. Three survived the fury of the reef and were helped ashore by Lawrence, who had returned to the beach, the others were washed out to sea and drowned.

On board the wreck several more attempts were made to get people ashore and a boat under the command of the chief officer capsized in the surf. Of the men in this boat all but one survived the ordeal and landed safely, the last, a fourteen-year-old-boy, was drowned.

These few who made it to shore and the crew of the second officer's boat, which stood off the reef until the next morning were the only ones, apart from one man who swam direct from the ship, that were saved from the 151 persons on board the *Tararua*.

During the second night on the reef the weather worsened with the waves sweeping over the doomed ship. The passengers and crew had all been taken to the fo'c'sle head and either climbed into the fore rigging or hung onto anything they could find while the water crashed over them; one by one they were washed from the ship and drowned.

Apart from the earlier two boats taken out by the first and second officers all had been smashed or washed from the ship and the plight of those left on board was desperate.

At two thirty in the morning the end came and after shrieks and cries from those still holding on to or lashed to the rigging there was silence. Of a total complement of 151 men, women and children, twenty survived the terrible ordeal at Waipapa Point.

The subsequent enquiry into the wrecking blamed the captain for being uncertain of his position, and the lookout who failed to see the breakers ahead in time – both died in the aftermath of the wreck. The court recommended that a light be placed on Waipapa Point and that all vessels should carry enough lifeboats to accommodate everyone on board – both recommendations were later adopted.

The *Tararua* had been in the news before her untimely wrecking, the first time it was also connected with treasure. In November 1880 the vessel sailed from Dunedin with eleven cases of gold on board; each case containing five gold bars worth £1,000 each and when she reached Hobart en route for Melbourne, a further case of gold was placed with the others in her strong-room aft.

Imagine the surprise and consternation of the officers, who had witnessed the consignment locked into the strong-room when, on being opened in Melbourne, it was found that one case worth £5,000 was missing. The ship was searched, the crew were followed by plainclothes detectives but the gold was not found. The captain had his master's certificate suspended and the crew were transferred to other vessels in the Union Company fleet, and still there was no sign of the missing bullion.

It was not until three years later when one of the stewards died that, on searching an old chest of his, the police found three of the five missing gold bars. The other two have never been recovered and it is not outside the realms of possibility that they were never taken off the *Tararua* and are still lying on the sea floor near the Waipapa Point reef.

On her last disastrous voyage the *Tararua* was again carrying bullion in her strong room. This time it was a consignment of old silver coins withdrawn from circulation by the New Zealand Government to be shipped back to England for re-minting. The exact value of this consignment seems to be in some doubt but is variously quoted as having been anything from £3,500 to £8,000. Not a vast treasure but the coins were silver and worth considerably more than the cupro-nickel coins of today. The fact that it was considered to be extremely valuable is borne out by later salvage attempts.

Within two weeks of the tragedy a Government commissioned ketch, the *Good Templar*, left Port Chalmers for the wreck site with a diver on board. Plagued by bad weather and heavy swells they did not stay long and, although the diver did descend to the *Tararua* and ascertained that she had broken into three pieces, he could not locate the bullion and the ketch returned to Port Chalmers with no treasure and minus a few anchors, a surfboat and a buoy, victims of the atrocious conditions.

It was to be eight years before salvage was resumed and after this period several attempts were made to recover the elusive silver over the next few years – all to no avail.

Rumours circulated that during the eight year break in operations pirates had

Many of the victims of the *Tararua* disaster were buried in Tararua Acre, a farmer's paddock near the wreck site. (Steve Locker-Lampson).

removed the contents of the bullion room. People said ships had been seen standing off the reef and that one vessel had, on several occasions, come towards the reef at dusk only to slip away again at dawn. Were these pirates or were they the excuses of the salvage crews for their inability to find the missing coins themselves? Considering the problems experienced by the authorised salvors it seems unlikely that pirates would succeed where stealth was all important. It is more likely that because of the ferocious seas and stormy weather that are normal in the area, the divers were unable to locate the strong room and that which it contained.

As well as the many thousands of dollars worth of silver known to have been aboard the *Tararua*, there is an unknown quantity of gold in the form of personal jewellery and money owned by the passengers and crew. As in the case of the ss *Wairarapa* wrecked thirteen years later, there are letters in existence inquiring about the personal possessions of some of the passengers who died when the *Tararua* came to grief off Waipapa Point. One survivor stated after the disaster that he had left behind in his cabin a bag containing forty gold pieces. Another survivor reported that when he rushed on deck after the initial impact he completely forgot that he had left a hundred sovereigns under his pillow; and these stories are only from two of the twenty survivors – imagine how many more could have come from the 131 less fortunate people!

Stories similar to these abound and there must be many gold coins scattered among the remains of the *Tararua*, and pre-1881 gold coins can be extremely valuable now.

Shortly after the disaster an auction was held of flotsam from the wreck which would have included stores, passenger's belongings and ship's fittings. One man who purchased a locked suitcase must have been overjoyed when he found, on opening it, that amongst other things it contained one hundred gold sovereigns.

In 1969 a group from the Southland Skindiving Club made several attempts to dive on the wreck using scuba equipment, but were thwarted by the elements just as effectively as the earlier 'hard hat' divers had been, and had to return empty-handed. In the 1970s Kelly Tarlton and John Dearling located the wreck and while diving on it discovered a concreted mass of iron with what Tarlton described as 'pay dirt' embedded in it, including coins, jewellery and at least one gold watch case. It was a large piece of concretion and the only way to move it as far as Tarlton could see was to break it up with a few small charges of explosive and then haul it to shore for the finer work of extracting the valuable objects. He made a very un-Tarlton-like mistake and the charges were larger than necessary destroying the concretion so utterly that the ferocious seas scattered the debris and the team could find no trace of the 'pay dirt' when they went back to collect the treasure!

It is believed that a substantial portion of the silver bullion was finally recovered in the late 1980s and, because these rumours are so consistent this is

John Dearling and Kelly Tarlton on the site of the *Tararua* with a few small items for the Shipwreck Museum. (John Dearling).

John Dearling with portholes from the wreck of the *Tararua*. (John Dearling).

probably the case. If someone has unearthed this elusive cargo then it was almost certainly done illegally or there would have been some publicity about it but no one, for obvious reasons, is prepared to put a name to who was responsible.

Regardless of whether the bulk of the silver was salvaged within a few years of the wreck or in much more recent times there is still a fortune down there near Waipapa Point, and although many more searches are likely to be made in the future, most of it will probably remain there forever. It is a rough and treacherous coast with rare calm days and anything other than almost dead flat water is not for the faint-hearted!

This wreck and its contents were bought by Kelly Tarlton from Joan MacIntosh, author of the book *The Wreck Of The Tararua*. The remains are now owned by Rosemary Tarlton.

A concreted mass of silver coins recovered from the *Tararua*. (Chris Glasson).

CHAPTER SEVEN

ELINGAMITE

The ss *Elingamite* leaving Wellington. (Dickie collection. Alexander Turnbull Library).

One of the more tragic wrecks associated with New Zealand was that of the *Elingamite*, sunk on 9 November, 1902 at the Three Kings Islands, north west of the extreme northern tip of the country. Inward bound to Auckland from Sydney, she was creeping through a thick fog at half speed when she steamed into West King Island and sank in deep water within twenty minutes. Of the 136 passengers and 58 crew on board at the time only 149 people eventually made it to Auckland. Forty five people died that fateful night and in the succeeding days; some drowning in the immediate aftermath of the wreck, some dying from exposure on one of the rafts that drifted away from the islands; and an unknown number who disappeared in one of the lifeboats – no trace of this boat or its complement was ever found.

The greatest tragedy in this particular wrecking was that the master, Captain Atwood, was on his correct course even though he was blamed for the accident at the Court of Enquiry and had his certificate suspended. It was not until eight years later that it was discovered that, in fact, the position of the Three Kings Islands was incorrectly shown on the chart and that, had this been accurate, the tragedy would never have happened. The amazing thing is that more vessels did not suffer the same fate as the islands are on the usual route between Sydney and Auckland and it is not uncommon for them to be shrouded in fog.

As far as treasure is concerned, the *Elingamite* is a classic treasure wreck; all the ingredients are there – bullion at the bottom of the sea, fruitless attempts to recover it, eventual partial recovery, divers dying for strange reasons, rumours of illegal salvage attempts and, finally, modern day methods triumphing over the forces of nature to wrest gold and silver from the sea floor – but by no means all of it.

The salvage story goes back a long way and has covered many years and there will be further attempts in the future, even if only by amateurs after a few coins – known treasure wrecks are rarely allowed to rest undisturbed.

At the time of her sinking the *Elingamite* was carrying £17,320 worth of bullion consisting of 6,000 half sovereigns, £14,300 worth of silver coin and £20 worth of copper coin. Not a particularly valuable cargo at face value but worth considerably more in 1902 than the modern equivalent in dollars. Today however, the value of the silver metal alone, one and a half tonnes of it, would be worth almost $500,000 and with half sovereigns fetching about $100 each the gold would be worth at least $600,000 without taking into account any rarity value they might have. Well over a million dollars altogether!

The first attempt to locate the wreck of the *Elingamite* and to search for the missing lifeboat was made ten days after her sinking but, although they found some of the wreckage thereby indicating the approximate position of the site, the ferocious seas prevented any diving being done. Finally they returned to Auckland without being able to pinpoint the wreck and not having found any trace of the missing boat.

Sea conditions at the West King are almost always bad with heavy swells crashing into the base of the cliffs and vicious currents and tide rips sweeping across the wreck site. For modern scuba divers the area is treacherous and extremely dangerous unless stringent safety precautions are observed and, combined with the depth of the wreck – approximately thirty to fifty metres – it is not a diving spot to be taken lightly. How much more difficult it must have been for the earlier 'hard-hat' divers with their bulky, cumbersome equipment and limited mobility; it is little wonder that several of the early potential salvors never managed to get a diver down to the wreck.

The next five expeditions to the site over the following three years, all with the intention of raising the bullion, were again thwarted by bad weather and although on a couple of occasions the divers managed to get under water they

A buoy, tied to the wreckage, marks the site of the *Elingamite* below the cliffs of West King Island. (Malcolm Blair).

never reached the main wreckage and all returned to New Zealand with nothing to show for their labours and considerably out of pocket.

The seventh attempt, in February 1906, managed to place a diver on the wreck itself on at least five occasions but, although he apparently searched as thoroughly as possible, he found no trace of the bullion and once again the salvage crew returned empty-handed.

The eighth try ended when the diver got into trouble on his first descent and ballooned to the surface with a blocked exhaust valve, being lucky not to lose his life from an embolism (the expansion of the air in his lungs as the outside pressure dropped during his ascent). He was, even so, an extremely sick man for some time and had to be quickly returned to the mainland.

It was not until the ninth attempt, in January 1907, that any of the *Elingamite's* bullion was seen above water. On this expedition, using the auxiliary schooner *Huia*, the diver was an extremely experienced man by the name of E. Harper and, over several dives, he sent to the surface about £1500 worth of the lost treasure including an unspecified quantity of gold.

After a few days break to allow a storm to pass, diver Harper went back to work and on one day made three descents sending to the surface a further £800 of which about £400 was in gold. On climbing back on board the *Huia* he was found to be in trouble and, although everything was tried in a effort to help him, he died soon afterwards of what was said at the time to be over exertion and a heart attack but what could have in fact been the 'bends' more properly known as decompression sickness. The bends are caused by diving too deep for too long and are the result of compressed nitrogen entering the blood stream in suspension while under pressure and forming into bubbles in the blood once the outside pressure is lowered during the diver's ascent. This diving problem is overcome nowadays by decompression stops on the way to the surface to allow time for the nitrogen to be dissipated. The length of the stops depends on the length of time that the diver has spent underwater and the depth he has attained.

Decompression tables detailing the length of stops and the depths at which they should be taken have been available now for many years but were not accurately formulated until after Harper died. Had he been diving to the modern tables he would have been quite safe had he decompressed on his first dive for a few minutes, on his second for at least half an hour and on his third for over two hours. He did none of this but was each time hauled straight to the surface and the outcome was inevitable. The *Elingamite* had taken her forty sixth life.

The next four salvage operations managed to raise another £1,200 worth of bullion but again ended in the death of the diver and again from the dreaded bends.

The total treasure taken from the vessel was, at this time, somewhere between £2½-3,000, leaving about £15,000 still underwater. Of the gold it would seem that about one thousand of the half sovereigns had been recovered, about five thousand of them were still on or near the wreck.

Between 1908 and 1957 there were a few half-hearted attempts for the *Elingamite's* remaining specie and another diver died from decompression sickness. There were also several rumours that it had been removed by unauthorised American or Australian salvors.

It was in March 1957 that the wreck site was first visited by a scuba diver. In that year Les Subritzki dived at the Three Kings and relocated the wreckage, collecting for himself a few souvenirs but not seeing any of the bullion. When he surfaced from the dive the current had swept him some distance from his boat and he was extremely fortunate that his sharp-eyed boatman spotted him before he was washed away from the area or dashed on the jagged rocks at the base of the cliff. He later said that he was glad that he had made the dive but that if there was any treasure on the *Elingamite* someone else was welcome to it – he did not want to dive there again.

Another ten years were to pass before anyone was again to see anything of the *Elingamite* and this time it was a group of keen spearfishermen who, knowing that the wreck was in the vicinity, decided to take a look. Surprisingly they found the wreckage almost immediately but, as it was their last dive of the trip they did not have time to explore the remains and returned to Auckland with every intention of visiting the site again.

A year later, in 1968, some of the same group, led by Kelly Tarlton and Wade Doak, returned to the wreck and, again on the last dive of the trip, Doak stumbled on the treasure. Being towards the end of his dive he had time to grab only a few pounds worth of coins before having to surface, but for him and Kelly Tarlton the search was on. They determined to try for the rest of the *Elingamite's* elusive bullion and after a short stop in Auckland, returned to the site to work the wreck properly.

This third try netted the syndicate a total of nearly four and a half thousand silver coins with a face value of approximately £300, and eleven half sovereigns – not a great deal but at least they had explored the wreck thoroughly and knew what they had to do to raise more of the booty.

Another year passed and, after extensive preparations, Tarlton and Doak once again set sail for the wreck site. This time they were better equipped and had gone prepared. They blasted the conglomerated masses of silver coins with explosives and hauled them up by the hundreds; they also blasted the bronze propeller blades from the boss and tried, without success to lift them. By the end of the trip they had raised over 10,000 silver coins and a few – a very few – half sovereigns.

In January 1969 they returned and again recovered some silver coins but this time their major prize was the four bronze propeller blades weighing over a tonne each – worth thousands of dollars as scrap they at least made the expedition profitable.

The treasure hunters examine silver coins from the *Elingamite* on the dive tender after an early expedition in the 1960s. (Kelly Tarlton).

Since 1969 sets of *Elingamite* coins have been sold by various means and these, together with other *Elingamite* souvenirs and items from a variety of other wrecks were the foundation of Kelly Tarlton's famous Museum of Shipwrecks on the converted sugar lighter, *Tui*, at Waitangi in the Bay of Islands.

In all, the Elingamite Syndicate headed by Doak and Tarlton recovered approximately 150kg of silver coins and twenty one half sovereigns from the wreck between 1966 and 1969. In addition numerous artifacts, including the ship's bell, were raised from their watery grave. The group did over one hundred and fifty dives to depths of approximately 50 metres and the fact that they never had a single accident in that time shows the extreme professionalism with which they went about their task.

Tarlton went back to the *Elingamite* site again in the summer of 1979-80 with a team of professional divers and a recompression chamber and, over several months, numerous silver coins and more half sovereigns were raised, but not the 'mother lode' of gold he had always been searching for.

The Three Kings is not an area to be taken lightly, it is not for the novice or faint-hearted. It should be treated by the diver with the respect due to a heaving swell and swift current and those that think that they know better will almost certainly die and add to the toll of the *Elingamite*.

Quite apart from anything else the vessel and her cargo are now owned outright by Rosemary Tarlton and it is illegal to remove anything from the wreck without her permission, regardless of whether it is a single silver shilling or a thousand half sovereigns.

In recent years there have been a few official expeditions to the site of the famous shipwreck as well as numerous illegal ones and an unknown amount of gold and silver has been recovered. Most 'pirate' groups of divers will have come away with a handful of coins as souvenirs but a few will have been more persistent in their search and may well have returned considerably better off than when they left. However, without a major expedition which could probably not be launched without the owners consent it is likely that a great deal of the specie is still in or near the *Elingamite's* shattered remains. The depth of water and the violent currents combined with the difficulty of locating anything other than the odd loose coin will make most of these trips financially fruitless.

From all available records it would seem that somewhere in the region of £6,000 worth of silver has been recovered together with close to 3,000 half sovereigns but that still leaves more than £8,000 worth of coins at their face value still on the sea floor. Their actual value today would be many times this figure!

Silver coins and one ½ sovereign from the bullion on the *Elingamite*. (Kelly Tarlton).

CHAPTER EIGHT

TASMANIA

The ss *Tasmania*, later to be wrecked off Mahia Peninsula. (Alexander Turnbull Library).

Although the weather was bad on the night of July 29, 1897 it was not for this reason that the Huddart Parker steamer *Tasmania* went aground off Mahia Peninsula but, according to the subsequent enquiry, through careless and negligent navigation on the part of the master and third officer.

Thirteen people lost their lives in the aftermath of the wreck, eleven of them from one lifeboat which capsized while trying to get ashore through the surf, and the vessel sank in thirty metres of water approximately five kilometres north of Mahia Peninsula, on the east coast of the North Island.

Of all the New Zealand treasure wrecks there is no doubt that the *Tasmania* holds one of the most successful records for salvage even though less than half of her treasure has yet been recovered.

Early in 1973 Kelly Tarlton set off to look for items for his Museum of Shipwrecks from the wreck of the *Tongariro*, sunk at Bull Rock, Mahia in 1916, and while he was there to try to locate the wreck of the *Tasmania*. His interest in the *Tasmania* was purely as another wreck that might yield a few artifacts for the hungry display cases on his converted sugar lighter, the *Tui*, and it was only when a local diver who knew the location refused to tell him where it was that he became suspicious and started researching it himself.

In March of the same year reporters unearthed the fact that the vessel had gone down with a considerable quantity of jewellery on board – but Tarlton was ahead of them and was already laying plans for an assault on the vessel.

Over the next few months he worked hard on researching the wreck and making preparations for a salvage attempt later in 1973 and endeavoured to sort out the problems of salvage rights and ownership of the jewellery, and it was not until November that he finally set off with a group of divers to try to wrest the treasure from the sea.

As always Kelly Tarlton had done his research well and knew that the jewellery had been en route from Auckland to Wellington with a jeweller, Mr I.J. Rothschild, who had been intending to sell his goods in Wellington. Although Mr Rothschild escaped from the wreck he neglected, by force of circumstance, to take his valuable suitcase of jewellery with him when he boarded the lifeboat.

An attempt to recover this suitcase was made by a 'hard-hat' diver shortly after the wreck but, on surfacing, he reported that he had been unable to reach Mr Rothschild's cabin because of the bodies of horses, that had been part of the cargo, blocking the alleyways. This would seem a rather poor excuse and does not explain why a further attempt was not made in later years when the carcasses of the horses would have decayed.

Mr Rothschild had several other ingenious ideas about salvage including one for raising the complete vessel by filling it with inflated balloons. (Interestingly enough this scheme anticipated modern salvage methods of raising wrecks by pumping them full of liquid polystyrene. The polystyrene would expand inside forcing the water out. This technique was originally to be used on the inter-island ferry *Wahine* which sank in Wellington Harbour with the loss of 51 lives, in 1968, during the worst storm ever recorded in New Zealand. However, while preparations were under way another severe storm struck Wellington a year later breaking the vessel into three parts and making this method of salvage impractical. The *Wahine* was eventually cut up and lifted piecemeal from the harbour floor to clear the shipping channel into the harbour.)

Tarlton was not sure but suspected that no further efforts had been made to recover the jewellery and he considered the gamble of an expensive salvage operation to be justified. His specially built salvage boat the *Discoverer II*, was fitted with 15cm suction dredges to remove the deep sand from the portion of the wreck where Rothschild's cabin had been and, although there was no certainty that they would find the treasure – or even that it was still on the wreck

Barry Crane and John Dearling with artifacts recovered from the *Tasmania*. (John Dearling).

– Tarlton was determined at any rate to "have a lot of fun".

When the *Tasmania* sank in 1897 the jewellery was valued at £3,000, not an inconsiderable sum at the time. In 1973 the value was estimated to be between $50,000 and $100,000, although it was probably much higher. Ownership of the valuables was an initial problem until Mr Rothschild's daughter was found living in Melbourne and was approached through Tarlton's solicitors. An agreement was reached between the two parties and Tarlton bought both the wreck and its contents, including the jewellery, for the sum of $3,000.

Three weeks after commencing the salvage attempt Tarlton believed that he was close to the area where Rothschild's cabin had been. He had removed the overburden of sand and reached the deck of the ship and calculated that what remained of the superstructure, including the cabin, should now be beside the hull of the vessel. More digging was required and the suction dredges were repositioned where Tarlton thought the most likely areas were.

Lack of time eventually beat the diving team before they had definitely located the right place but Tarlton did not go home empty-handed. Many artifacts had been recovered for his Museum of Shipwrecks and shortly before calling off the search the team had found a few pieces of gold jewellery – could this be a sign of things to come or was it just lost items of jewellery from some of the other passengers?

During November 1974 Tarlton again took a team to Mahia for a second attempt at the Rothschild jewellery and after five weeks returned to Auckland with five small items that must surely have come from the elusive suitcase. One small gold piece for each week's diving. Certainly not enough to have made the trip financially successful but, equally certainly, an exquisite display for his museum and enough to keep Tarlton satisfied until he could return. Now he knew that he was in the right area of the wreck and he determined to continue the search in April 1975.

April and May of 1975 proved as frustrating as the previous expedition and, even though Tarlton had designed and built a bigger, more efficient suction dredge, the results of the three weeks work were hugely disappointing. Frequently held up by bad weather the diving team only recovered a few gold trinkets believed to have belonged to Rothschild and finally had to again return to their normal jobs.

However, it was difficult to restrain Kelly Tarlton once he had got his teeth into something in which he believed and by November 1975 he was back once again, more determined than ever to recoup some of the money that he had poured into the venture, and this time his faith in himself and his diving team paid off. Three weeks after arriving at the wreck site they had recovered almost a hundred pieces of jewellery. Their best day saw thirty five pieces brought back into the light of day. Tarlton was a happy man.

Some of the recovered items were magnificent and extremely valuable but

A beautiful brass mirror frame found on the *Tasmania*. (Kelly Tarlton).

Tarlton was not interested in selling them. Apart from a few pieces given away to members of his team he determined to keep the rest for display in his museum at Waitangi. Among the items were rings, brooches, fob chains, watch cases, opals and greenstone. Rubies and diamonds glittered among the pile of gold.

These trips were no diving holiday and apart from sucking away sand and mud from the wreck with the jet unit the divers were forced to blast and remove large sections of steel that were lying in the area in which Tarlton thought he would find more of the jewellery. Storms were frequent, problems with the salvage boat occurred all too often and the divers several times suffered from mild cases of the 'bends'. Tarlton himself had the worst case and was probably only saved from permanent injury by getting his diving crew to put his gear back on him and take him back to the bottom, in over 31 metres of water, where he waited for a few minutes before slowly, over one and a half hours, returning to the surface. This is not a recommended way of treating decompression sickness but worked admirably in this instance and Tarlton was left with no ill effects.

In 1982 he again set off to the wreck site with a group of experienced divers and with backing from an Australian syndicate. He found the mud on the wreck had come back in over the previous six years and was over two metres higher than when he had last seen it. With a new suction dredge it was no great problem to move this but it took time and when they eventually cleared a crater five metres deep they came across steel plates – six layers of them – and these had to be carefully blasted and lifted from the site.

After spending ten weeks on the *Tasmania* Tarlton eventually admitted that he was beaten. He had only recovered 53 pieces of jewellery and an undisclosed number of these were handed over to the Australian investors before he deposited the remainder in his Museum of Shipwrecks where they still remain. He always intended to go back to the wreck at some stage but his untimely death from a heart attack on 17 March, 1985 forestalled the realisation of this dream.

An estimate of the amount of jewellery still on the rotting remains of the *Tasmania* would be something over half of what was lost in 1897 and worth many thousands of dollars, but to locate and recover it is going to be no easy matter. Tarlton estimated that it had cost around $48,000 for his 1982 expedition and all he had found was 53 pieces of jewellery, an average cost per piece of over $900! The depth of the water, the conditions on the bottom, the state of the wreck and the frequent storms in the area will preclude the efforts of most dive groups, and unless it is an authorised endeavour it will be almost impossible to mount a major expedition where secrecy is all important. The vessel itself and the unrecovered jewellery are still owned outright by Rosemary Tarlton.

Nevertheless, the treasure of the *Tasmania* has almost certainly not seen the last of the salvage attempts – a known treasure will be hunted down the years until there is not enough left to make it profitable.

BIBLIOGRAPHY

NEW ZEALAND SHIPWRECKS (6th ed.), by CWN Ingram, AH & AW Reed, 1984.

THE WRECK BOOK (2nd Ed.), by Steve Locker-Lampson & Ian Francis, Halcyon Press, 1994.

THE BURNING OF THE BOYD, by Wade Doak, Hodder & Stoughton, 1984.

EIGHT MINUTES PAST MIDNIGHT, by Steve Locker-Lampson & Ian Francis, Rowfant Books, 1981.

GOLD FROM THE SEA, by James Taylor, Australian Publishing Company, 1942.

NIAGARA GOLD, by R.J. Dunn, AH & AW Reed, 1942.

THE WRECK OF THE GENERAL GRANT, by Keith Eunson, AH & AW Reed, 1974.

THE WRECK OF THE TARARUA, by Joan MacIntosh, AH & AW Reed, 1970.

THE ELINGAMITE AND ITS TREASURE, by Wade Doak, Hodder & Stoughton, 1969.

KELLY, by E.V .Sale, Reed Books, 1988.

COASTS OF TREACHERY, by Eugene Grayland, AH & AW Reed, 1963

LOST TREASURES IN AUSTRALIA & NEW ZEALAND, by Keneth Byron, AH & AW Reed, 1965.

AUSTRALIAN AND NEW ZEALAND SHIPWRECKS AND SEA TRAGEDIES by Hugh Edwards, Mathews/Hutchinson, 1978.

THE BLACK RAIDER, by Kurt Weyher & Hans Jurgen Ehrlich, Elek Books, 1955.

GERMAN RAIDERS OF THE SOUTH SEAS, by Robin Bromby, Doubleday, 1985.